ECDL®

European Computer Driving Licence®

ECDL Project Planning
BCS ITQ L2 Project Management Software

Using Microsoft® Project® 2013

Syllabus Version 1.0

This training, which has been approved by BCS, The Chartered Institute for IT, includes exercise items intended to assist learners in their training for an ECDL Certification Programme. These exercises are not ECDL certification tests. For information about Approved Centres in the UK please visit the BCS website at www.bcs.org/ecdl.

Release ECDL304_UKv2

Published by: CiA Training Ltd
Business & Innovation Centre
Sunderland Enterprise Park
Sunderland
SR5 2TA
United Kingdom

Tel: +44 (0) 191 549 5002
Fax: +44 (0) 191 549 9005

E-mail: info@ciatraining.co.uk
Web: www.ciatraining.co.uk

ISBN: 978-0-85741-192-1

This guide was written for *Microsoft Project 2013* running on *Windows*. If using a different version of *Office* some features and dialog boxes may not look and function exactly as described.

Project 2013 is optimised to work with touch-screen controls and online file storage. However, this guide assumes you are using a traditional mouse and keyboard and save your files locally.

A screen resolution of *1024x768* is also assumed. Working at a different resolution (or with an application window which is not maximised) may change the look of the dynamic *Office 2013 Ribbon*. For example, if space is restricted, a group of buttons may be replaced by a single button which, when clicked, will display the full group.

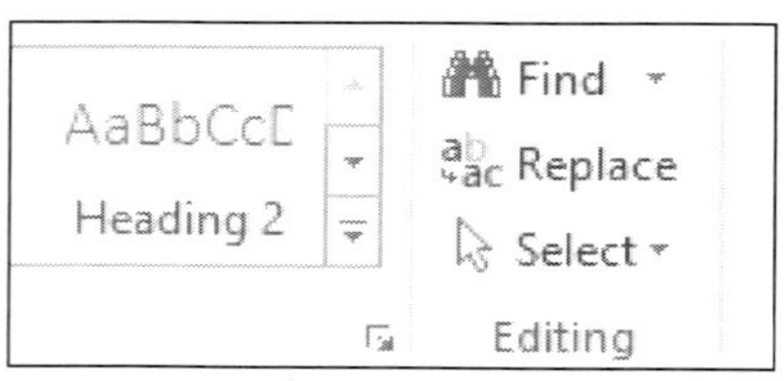

First published 2014.

ECDL | **BCS, The Chartered Institute for IT**
APPROVED COURSEWARE

This courseware may be used to assist learners to prepare for the ECDL Certification Programme as titled on the courseware. Neither BCS nor **CiA Training Ltd** warrants that the use of this courseware publication will ensure passing of the tests for that ECDL Certification Programme.

This courseware publication has been independently reviewed and approved by BCS as covering the learning objectives for the ECDL Certification Programme.

Confirmation of this approval can be obtained by reviewing www.bcs.org/ecdl.

The material contained in this courseware publication has not been reviewed for technical accuracy and does not guarantee that candidates will pass the test for the ECDL Certification Programme.

Any and all assessment items and/or performance-based exercises contained in this courseware relate solely to this publication and do not constitute or imply certification by BCS or ECDL Foundation in respect of the ECDL Certification Programme or any other ECDL test.

Irrespective of how the material contained in this courseware is deployed, for example in a learning management system (LMS) or a customised interface, nothing should suggest to the candidate that this material constitutes certification or can lead to certification through any other process than official ECDL certification testing.

For details on sitting a test for an ECDL certification programme in the UK, please visit the BCS website at www.bcs.org/ecdl.

Learners using this courseware must be registered with BCS before undertaking a test for ECDL. Without a valid registration, the test(s) cannot be undertaken and no certificate, nor any other form of recognition, can be given to a learner. Registration should be undertaken with BCS at an Approved Centre.

Downloading the Data Files

Data files accompanying this guide allow you to learn and practise new skills without the need for lots of data entry. These files must be downloaded from the Internet. Go to **www.ciatraining.co.uk/data** and follow the simple on-screen instructions.

Your *FastCode* for this guide's data is: **ECDL304**

The data files should be installed in the following location on your computer:

Documents \ DATA FILES \ ECDL \ Project Planning

Aims

The aim of this guide is to provide you with the practical skills required to use project management software to create and monitor project plans. Additional learning objectives also include managing time, costs, tasks and resources.

Objectives

After completing this guide you will be able to:

- Understand key concepts relating to managing projects
- Use a project management application to create a new project
- Use a project management application to update and maintain an existing project
- Create and schedule tasks and add project constraints and deadlines
- Create and assign costs and resources
- View the critical path, monitor progress and reschedule work
- Prepare and print outputs such as Gantt charts and reports.

Assessment of Knowledge

At the end of this guide is a **Record of Achievement Matrix**. Before the guide is started, it is recommended that you complete the matrix to measure your current level of knowledge. After working through a section, return to and update the **Record of Achievement**. Only when you feel you are competent in all areas should you move on to the next section.

Contents

Section 1
Getting Started

By the end of this section you should be able to:

Understand the concepts of project management

Start Project

Create a new project plan

Set up a plan

Adjust the working week

Recognise screen features

Use help

Work through the **Driving Lessons** in this section to gain an understanding of the above features.

For each **Driving Lesson**, read all of the **Park and Read** instructions and then, if applicable, perform the numbered steps of the **Manoeuvres**. Complete the **Revision** exercise(s) at the end of the section to test your knowledge.

Driving Lesson 1 - Project Management

Park and Read

The term **project** is used to describe any activity with a clear start and end that produces a result of some kind (e.g. a new product or service). Most projects are bound by time, resources and the type of results required.

***Resources** are the people, materials and equipment needed for a project. Managing projects involves constantly balancing resources, time and costs.*

To make sure that a project is achieved successfully, it must be planned and managed effectively. To do this, a **project plan** is often created. This breaks a large project down into a more manageable sequence of smaller **tasks** that are easier to understand and organise. The project plan is then used to guide, track and review a project's progress.

In general, the project management process can be divided into three phases:

1. The creation of a project plan

Firstly, the broad goals of a project need to be determined and then broken up into stages, deliverables and work packages. When will the project start and end and what are the desired outcomes? The focus at this point should be on the planned results of the project rather than the work needed to produce them.

Next, each stage of the project should be subdivided into individual tasks. The duration of each task should be estimated before working out their sequence: which tasks need to be completed before others and which tasks can be carried out simultaneously. Resources must also be assigned to the project; who will work on each task, what equipment is needed, and how much will it cost?

The next step is to set a schedule: create an availability, workday and holiday schedule for all resources. Once this is done, review the plan you have made, verifying its accuracy and completeness. You may also like to circulate the plan for review by others involved in the project.

2. Management of the project plan and schedule

Once the project starts, it is important to continually track real-world progress and review, adjust and improve the project plan accordingly. More importantly, the project plan should be used to look for potential problems (e.g. tasks taking longer than planned). These problems can be addressed by bringing in more help, substituting resources or rearranging tasks as required.

3. The communication of project information

Effective communication is vital during any project. Create reports for various aspects of the project and circulate these reports for review. Initiate meetings to revise and update the current project plan. Take action on the results of these meetings and revise the project plan accordingly.

Driving Lesson 2 - Microsoft Project

Park and Read

To help make the process of project management easier, computer software can be used to plan a project from start to end. Known as **project management software**, it can help you to design and maintain an effective and efficient project plan.

Microsoft Project is a popular choice of project management software. As you will learn in this guide, it can help you to organise project tasks, monitor their performance and costs, and allocate, balance and manage resources (i.e. people and equipment). The project plans created using this software can also be represented visually and a variety of useful reports can be generated.

Manoeuvres

1. Start your computer and log on to *Windows*.
2. Click once on the **Start** button (found towards the bottom left of the **Desktop** on the **Taskbar**). The **Start Menu** appears.

If you are using Windows 8, *a full **Start Screen** may appear instead.*

3. Click **All Programs** at the bottom of the **Start Menu** to show a list of available programs.

*In Windows 8, the **All Programs** button may appear as a downwards facing arrow.*

4. Within the **Microsoft Office 2013** folder, find and click the entry for the project management program **Project 2013**. You may need to scroll to find it. *Project* starts.

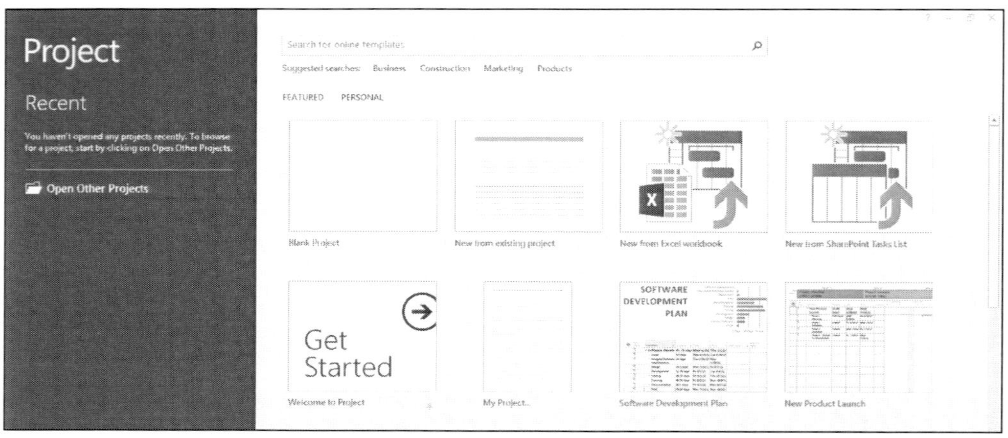

*You can also type **Project** on the **Start Menu** or **Start Screen** to search for and start the program.*

Driving Lesson 2 - Continued

*If this is the first time you have used Project, a **Welcome to Project** screen may appear. Feel free to explore this if you wish, then click the **FILE** tab and select **Close**. Click **No** if you are prompted to save changes.*

5. Before you continue, you also need to know how to close *Project*. To do this, simply click the **Close** button, ☒, in the top right corner once. Do this now.

If a project file is open when you close Project, *you may be prompted to save changes before closing. You will see this in practice later.*

6. *Project* is closed and is no longer running. Start *Project* again.

7. A list of recently used projects and templates is displayed on the default **Project** screen. You will explore many of the features available here later.

8. For now, click the **Blank Project** icon once.

You can use this technique at any time to create a new, blank project.

9. A new project is created and displayed. Move on to the next lesson.

Driving Lesson 3 - The Project Screen

Park and Read

Project displays information using various different views. The default view shows a list of project tasks on the left and a **Gantt Chart** on the right.

A Gantt Chart is a type of bar chart that visualises a project and shows tasks as horizontal bars on a timeline. Each bar is a task, and the start, end and length of the bar indicates its duration.

Manoeuvres

1. The *Project* screen will be similar to that shown below. Use the captions to identify some of the main features.

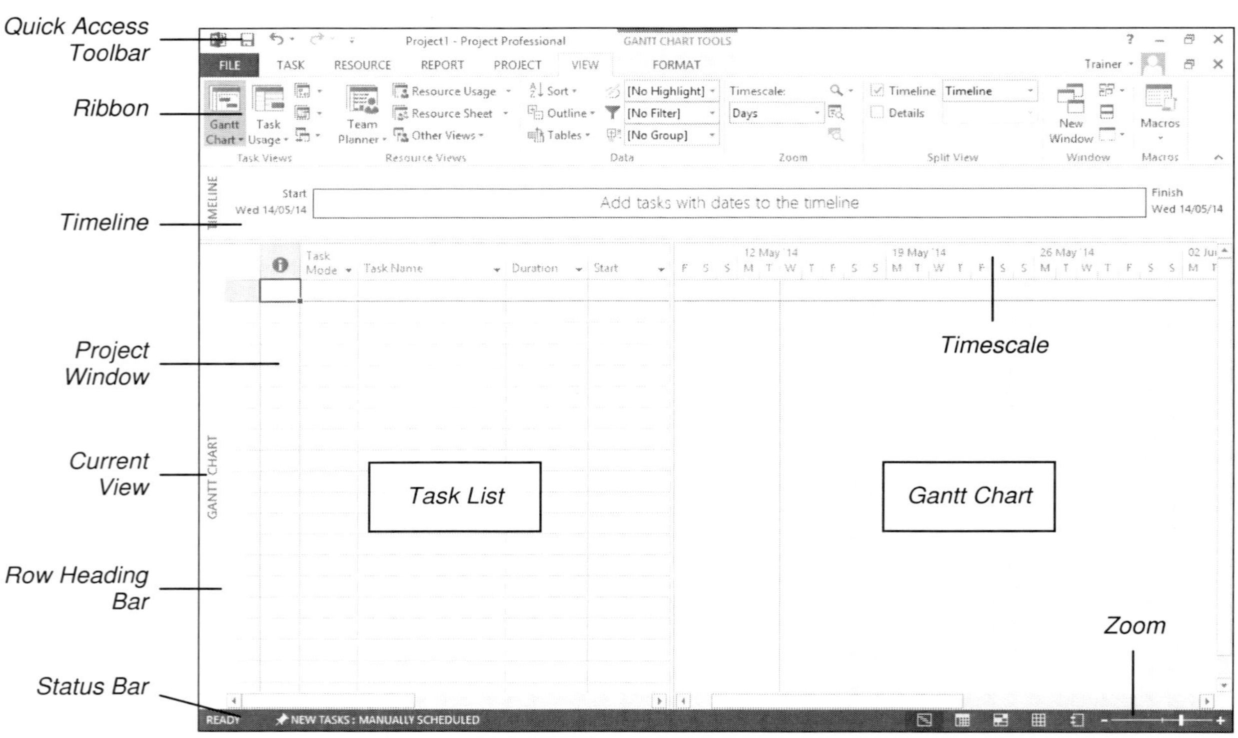

2. Locate the **Quick Access Toolbar** which contains a few popular command buttons. By default, this toolbar has three buttons, **Save**, **Undo** and **Redo**. This toolbar can be customised by adding further buttons.

3. Underneath the **Quick Access Toolbar** is the **Ribbon**. This is used to access the many features of *Project*, which you will learn more about in the next lesson.

4. Locate the **Timeline**. This can be used to show a quick visual snapshot of important tasks (and their progress). Its contents can also be copied and pasted into other *Office* programs.

Driving Lesson 3 - Continued

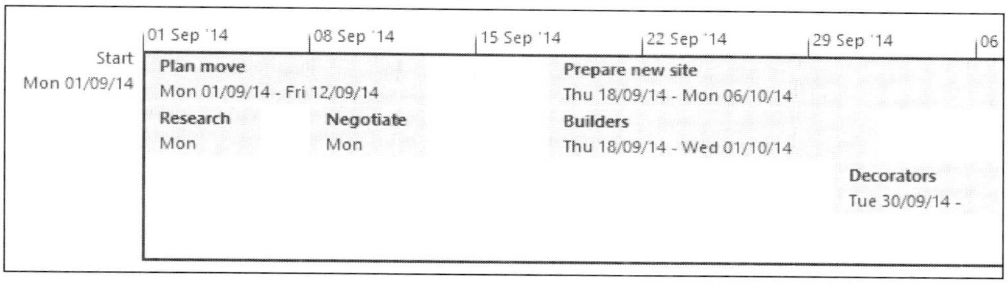

An example ***Timeline***

5. Notice that the **Project Window** is divided into two areas: a **Task List** where the details of each task in a project is shown, and a **Gantt Chart** which shows these tasks as bars on the project calendar.

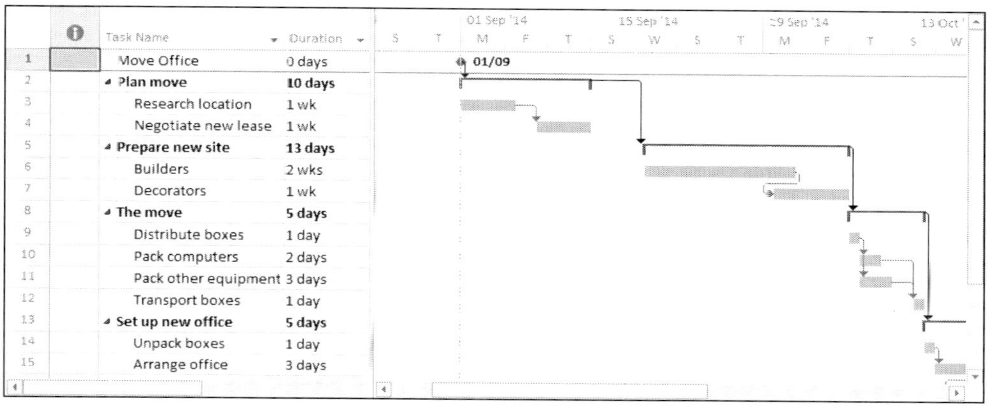

An example ***Gantt Chart***

6. The **Timescale** at the top of the **Gantt Chart** shows dates in the calendar. Notice that today's date is shown as a vertical green bar.

You can adjust pane sizes by dragging the boundary bar between them.

7. Find the **Status Bar** which runs along the bottom of the *Project* window. This displays useful messages as tasks are performed.

8. The **Zoom** slider to the right side of the **Status Bar** can be used to increase or decrease zoom levels in the **Gantt Chart**. You will get the opportunity to use this later.

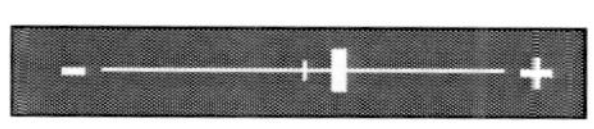

9. Leave *Project* open for the next lesson.

Driving Lesson 4 - The Ribbon

Park and Read

The **Ribbon** is displayed across the top of the *Project* window. It contains buttons and drop-down lists that can be used to control many of *Project*'s features.

Manoeuvres

1. Locate the **Ribbon**. This consists of a range of tabs containing buttons organised into groups.

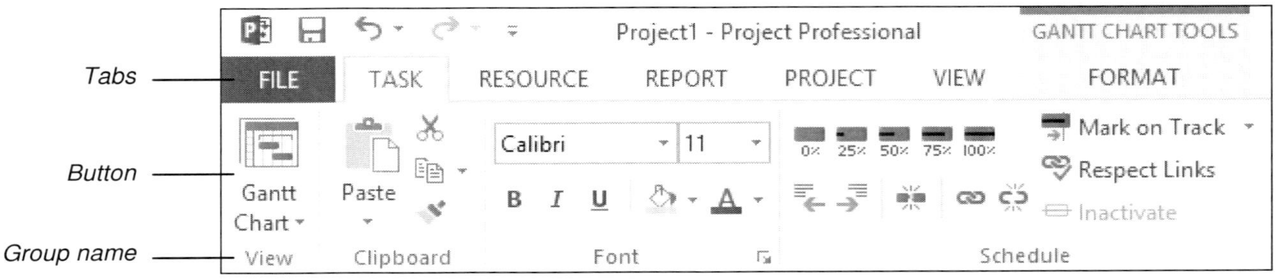

2. The buttons on the **Ribbon** are used to select an action or command in *Project*. Move the mouse pointer over any button but do not click. Read the **ToolTip** that appears which gives the name of that button and a small description.

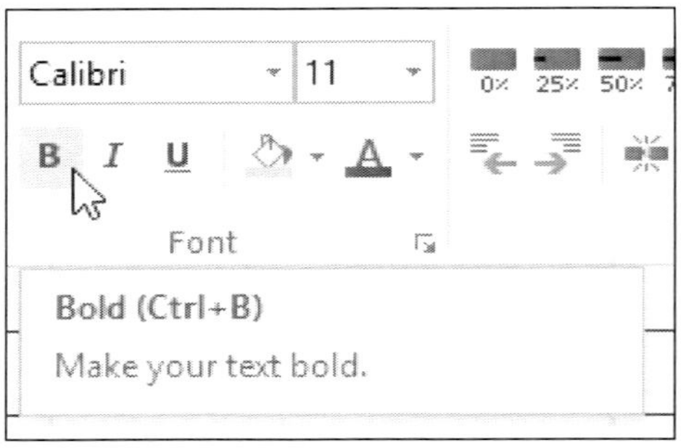

3. Click each tab at the top of the **Ribbon** in turn and examine the various features available. When you are finished, return to the **TASK** tab.

*The special **FILE** tab contains a list of basic program functions such as **Info**, **Open**, **Save**, **Save As**, **Print** and **Exit**. More advanced* Project *options can also be accessed from here.*

4. Most tabs are selected manually, but some will only appear when certain features are active. For example, as the **Gantt Chart** view is currently selected, the **GANTT CHART TOOLS - FORMAT** tab is displayed

Any buttons displayed in pale grey are inactive (or "ghosted") and are not available to be selected at present.

Driving Lesson 5 - Custom Views

Park and Read

There are many different ways to customise the *Project* screen. For example, you can resize the **Task List** and **Gantt Chart** or hide the **Ribbon** and **Timeline** to increase space in the **Project Window**.

Manoeuvres

1. Locate the **Collapse the Ribbon** button, , at the far bottom right of the **Ribbon**.

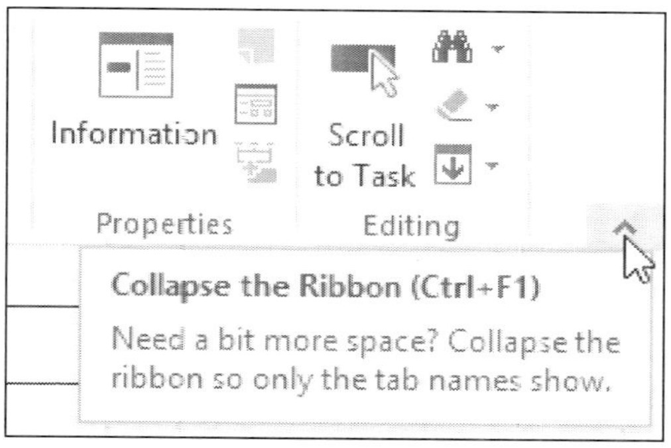

2. Click this once and the **Ribbon** is hidden. Notice that the **Ribbon's** tab headers are still visible at the top of the screen.
3. Clicking a tab header will temporarily show the **Ribbon**. Click **TASK** to view that tab, then click anywhere in the **Project Window** to hide it again.
4. Click the **TASK** tab to display the **Ribbon** again. Then, click the **Pin the ribbon** button, , to keep the **Ribbon** on-screen at all times again.

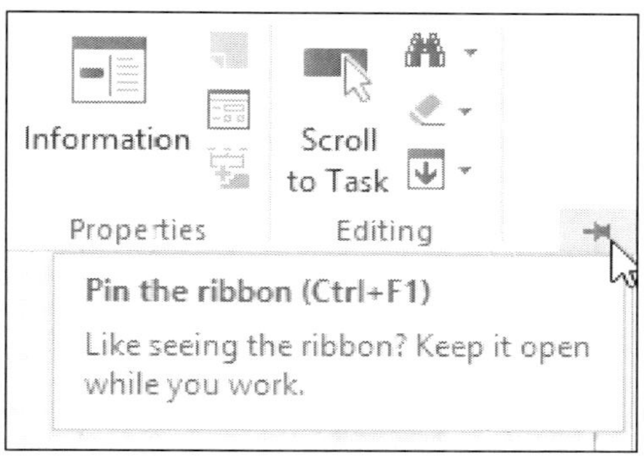

5. Next, display the **VIEW** tab. In the **Split View** group, remove the tick from the **Timeline** checkbox. Notice that the **Timeline** is hidden. This feature is not needed right now and hiding it gives you more room to work in.
6. Examine the buttons in the **Task Views** group. These allow you to view a project in different ways. Click **Task Usage** (click the button's icon, not the drop-down arrow). The screen's view changes.

Driving Lesson 5 - Continued

7. Try **Network Diagram** and **Calendar** also (click the buttons' icons, not their drop-down arrows). As your project is currently empty, there will be little to see on these screens right now.

You will return to these views later.

8. For now, click the **Gantt Chart** button's icon to return to the default view.

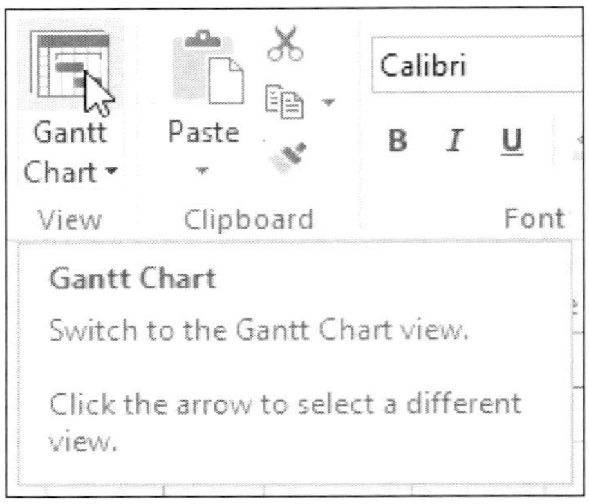

9. As you have already learned, the **Gantt Chart** view is split into two main areas: a **Task List** and the **Gantt Chart** itself. How this space is divided between the two areas can be changed. Place your mouse pointer over the dividing bar between the **Task List** and **Gantt Chart**.

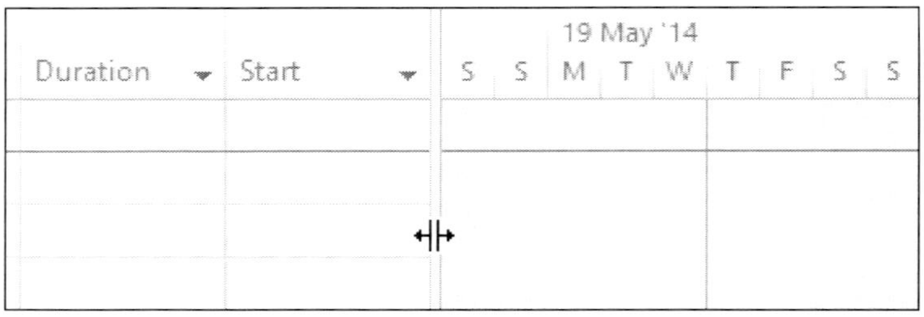

10. The mouse pointer changes to, ⟛. Click and drag the dividing bar a little to the right to increase the space occupied by the **Task List**. Notice that more columns are revealed in the **Task List**.

11. Try dragging the dividing bar a little way to the left – past halfway – to increase the space occupied by the **Gantt Chart**.

12. For now, place the dividing bar so that **Duration** is the last column header visible before the **Gantt Chart** appears.

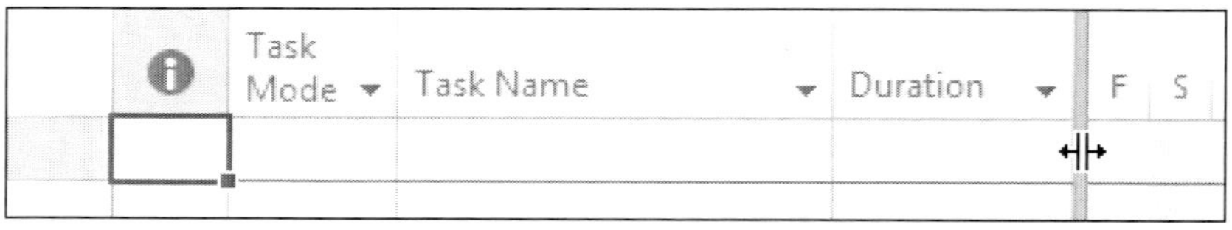

In practice, you can arrange your screen however you like it. For this guide, however, these recommended settings will be ideal.

Driving Lesson 6 - Help

Park and Read

Project contains a very useful and comprehensive **Help** facility. If you forget how to use a feature of the program or encounter an unexpected problem, this extra source of information can be very useful.

Help topics are available from either **Office.com** (via the Internet) or from the content installed on your computer (offline). The method of using **Help** is the same in either case but the content may vary slightly.

Manoeuvres

1. Click the **Help** button, ?, found to the far right of the **Title Bar**, to display the **Project Help** window.

*Pressing the <**F1**> key will display the same **Project Help** window. The window can be moved, resized or maximised if required.*

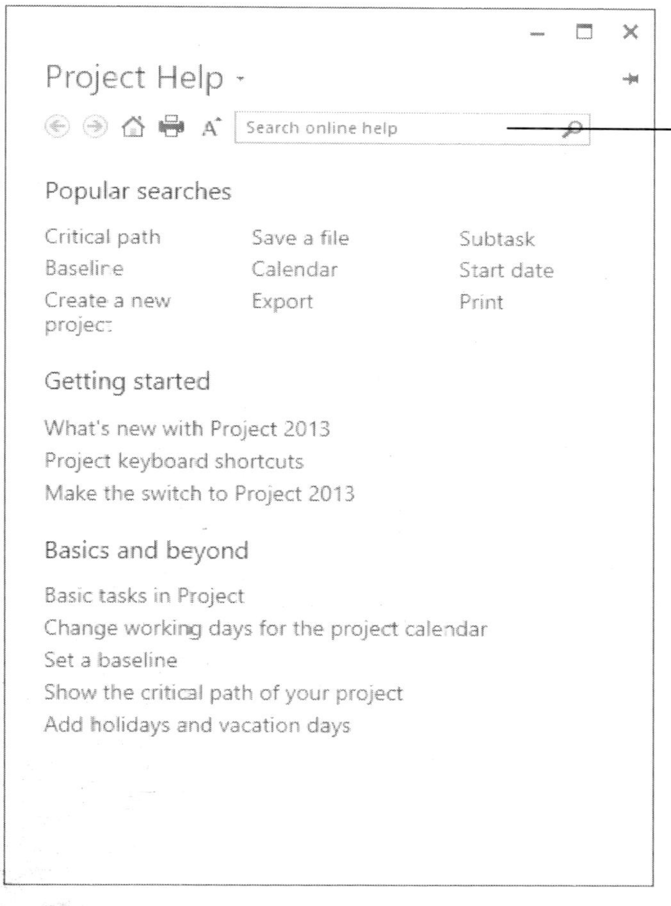

Search Box

*As the help screen downloads live content from **Office.com**, the contents may not appear exactly as shown above.*

Driving Lesson 6 - Continued

2. A list of **Popular searches** is shown on the opening screen. Click on any one that is of interest to you to display a list of relevant topics.

3. Scan the topics shown and select any one that you find interesting. Read the help information shown.

4. To move back to a previous screen, click the **Back** button, , on the **Project Help** toolbar. You are then able to follow another link.

5. Click the **Home** button, , on the toolbar to return directly to the starting help screen.

6. Another way to find help is to search by keyword. Type **toolbars** into the **Search online help** box and press <**Enter**>.

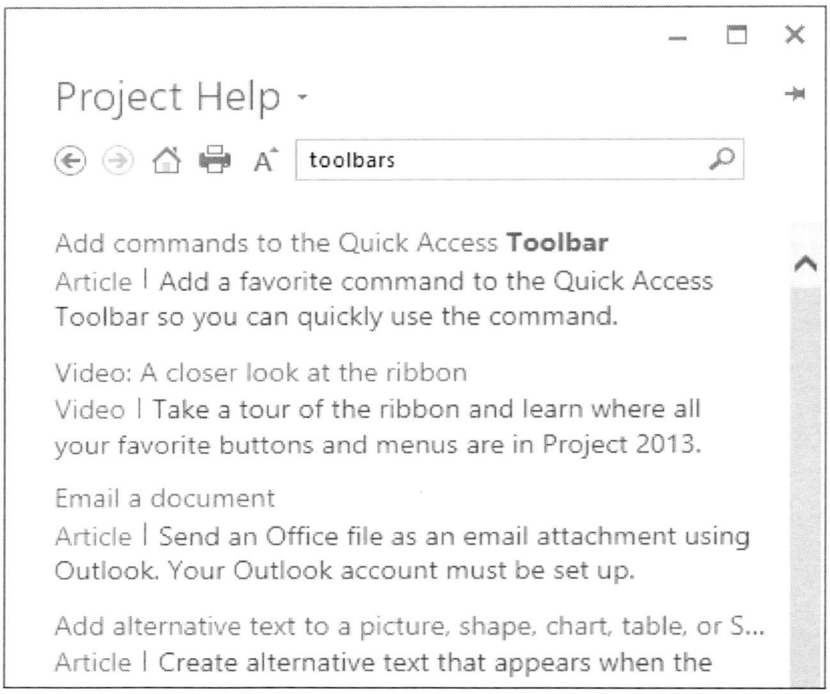

There may be many topics found for your search. It will be necessary for you to use your own judgement and select the most appropriate one.

7. Scan the topics found and again select any one that interests you. Read the help information shown.

8. Try searching for information on **keyboard shortcuts**. Find an appropriate article and read the useful information shown.

9. When you are finished, click the **Close** button, , on the **Project Help** box to close it (not the close button on the *Project* window)

Driving Lesson 7 - Project Information

Park and Read

Making Movies

Throughout this guide you will build a complete project plan to manage the development and filming of a movie. This type of project has been chosen so that you can easily understand the tasks that need to be carried out.

When starting a new project plan, it is best to enter **Project Information** first. This sets up important details such as the project's **Start date** and **Finish date**.

Manoeuvres

1. Display the **PROJECT** tab and click the **Project Information** button to display the **Project Information** dialog box.
2. Notice that the date in the **Start date** box is currently selected. Enter **01/01/2017** as the new start date for the project.

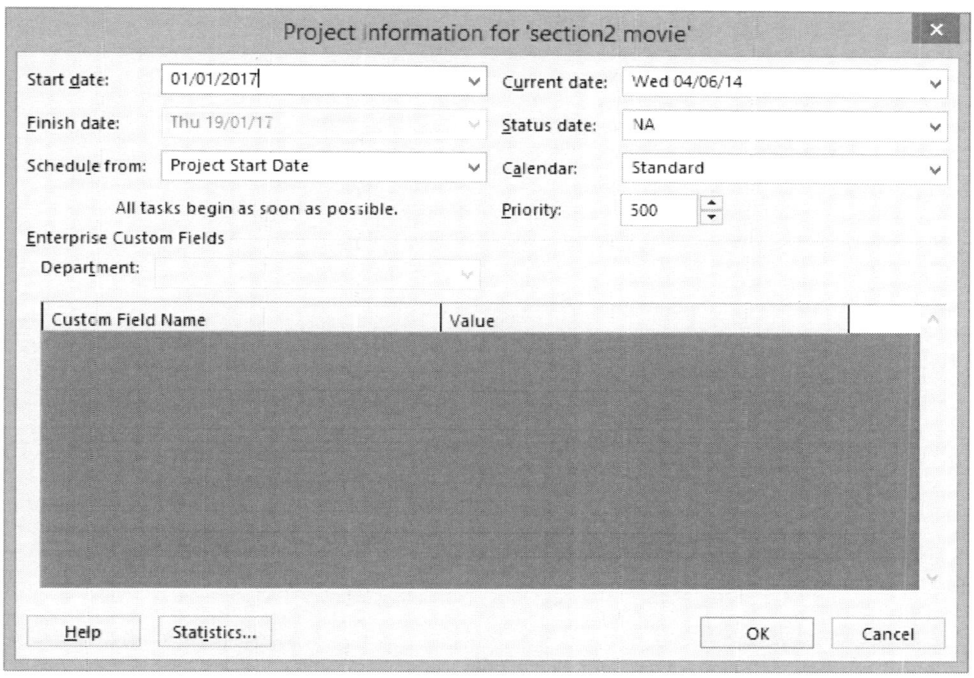

Don't worry if any dates used in this guide occur far in the future or in the past – this will not affect how you create and use the project plans described.

*If your project has a fixed deadline that you must meet, advanced users may prefer to set a **Finish date** instead and work backwards. To do this, you will need to select **Project Finish Date** from the **Schedule from** box first.*

Driving Lesson 7 - Continued

3. Click **OK** to accept the changes. Notice that the **Gantt Chart's** timescale changes to show a project starting on January 01, 2017.

*You can also add additional project title, author, manager and company information using the **Properties** dialog box.*

4. Click the **FILE** tab, 

, to show the **Info** screen. Click **Project Information**, displayed on the right of the screen.

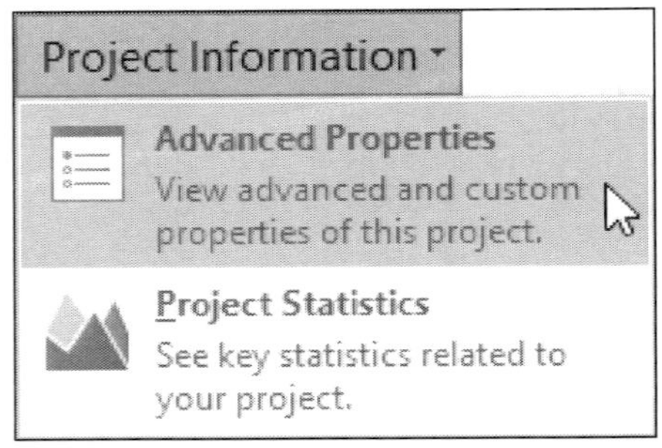

5. Select **Advanced Properties** from the drop-down list to display the **Properties** dialog box.
6. Click the **Summary** tab, if not displayed, to view an overview of project information.
7. These fields are optional and text can be added or omitted (**Title** will be automatically added when you save the project later). Enter **My Movie** in the **Subject** box and your name in the **Author** and **Manager** boxes.
8. Enter **CiA Pictures** in the **Company** box.

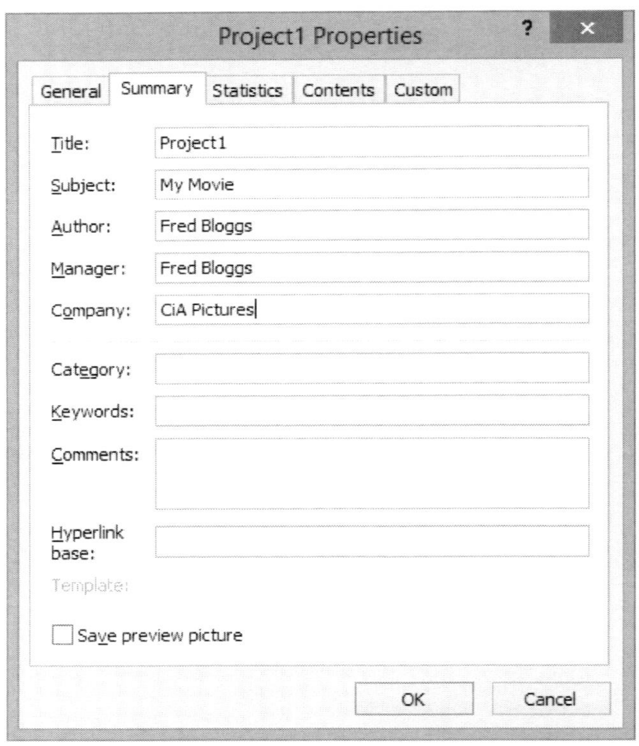

9. Click **OK** to save the information and then click **Back**, , in the top left corner of the **Info** screen.
10. Leave the unsaved project open for the next lesson.

Driving Lesson 8 - Working Times

Park and Read

Calendar options must be set up for each project and this is best done before adding tasks. Working and non-working time can be specified on the calendar.

Manoeuvres

1. On the **PROJECT** tab, click **Project Information** and, in the dialog box that appears, click the **Calendar** drop down arrow.

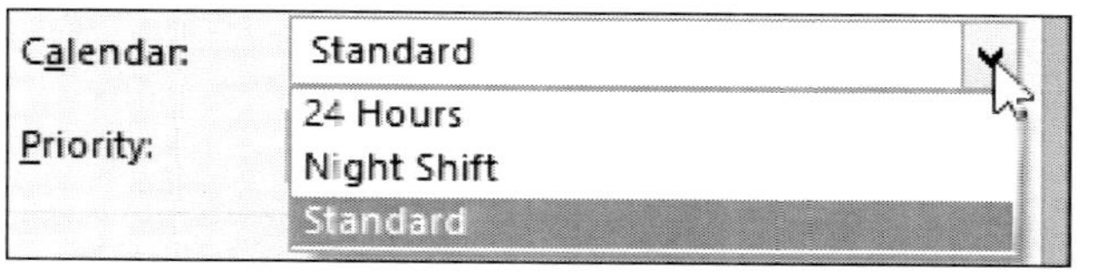

2. Notice that you can select calendar types for different working patters, i.e. **24 Hours** or **Night Shift**. For now, leave the **Calendar** as **Standard** (which is ideal for a normal working day) and click **OK**.

3. Next, click the **Change Working Time** button in the **Properties** group to set up the working week.

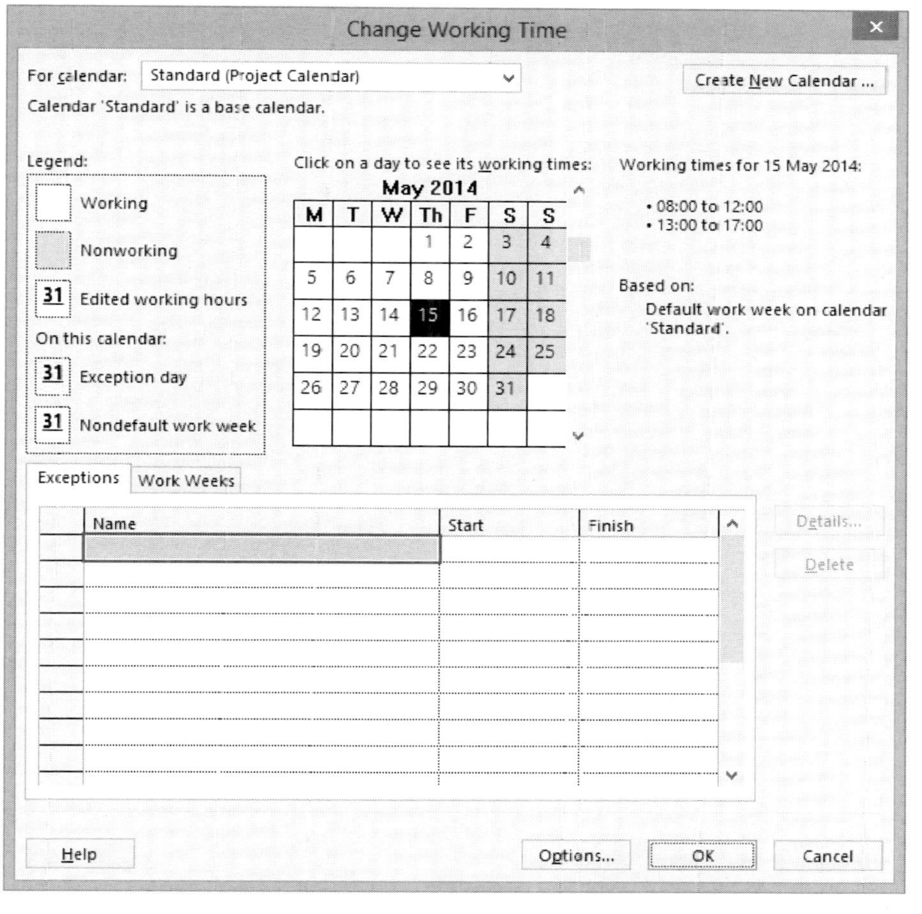

Driving Lesson 8 - Continued

4. Examine the **Legend** which shows the different types of day, including **Working** and **Nonworking** (i.e. weekends). These are used on the calendar which currently shows today's date.

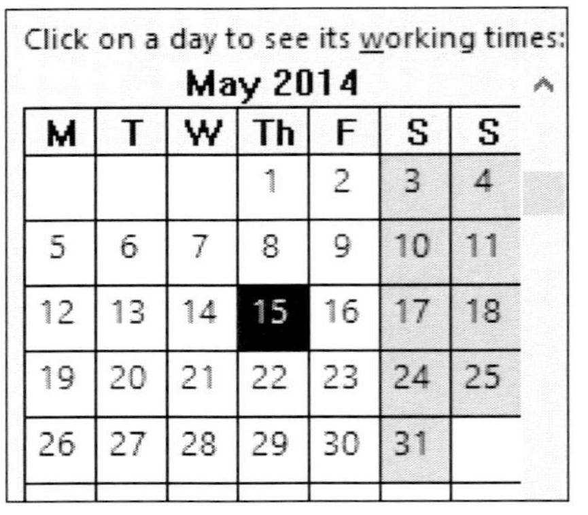

*Non-working days are shown in grey. Special nonworking days (i.e. holiday time) can be entered in the **Exceptions** tab at the bottom of the dialog box.*

5. Try selecting different dates on the calendar and notice the **Working times** that appear on the right.

6. Saturday mornings are to be worked on this project. Display the **Work Weeks** tab at the bottom of the dialog box and then click **Details**.

7. Select **Saturday** from the **Select day(s)** list and then select the option to **Set day(s) to these specific working times:**

8. Enter **09:00** in the first row under **From** and, under **To**, enter **13:00**.

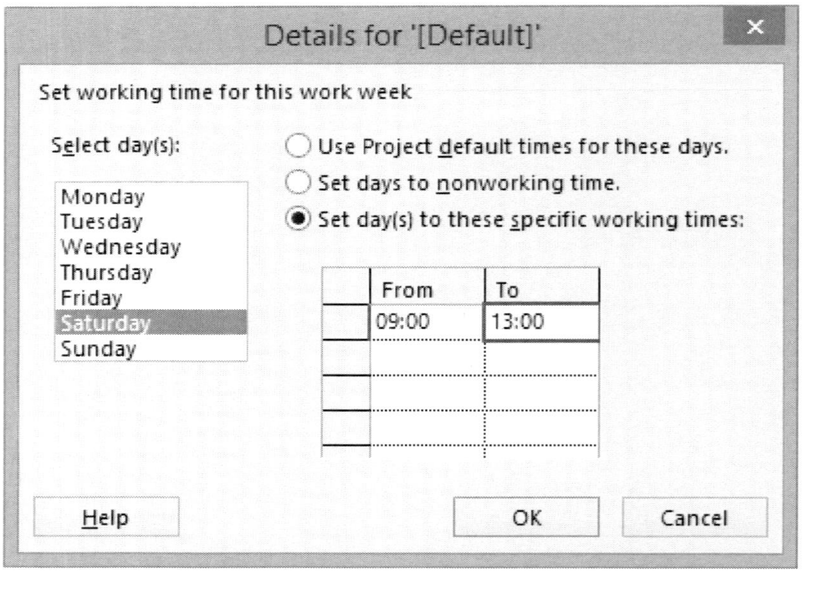

9. Click **OK** and Saturdays are now shown as work days. Select any day that falls on a Saturday in the calendar and notice the new **Working times**.

10. Click **OK** to save your new working week.

Driving Lesson 9 - Revision

Park and Read

At the end of every section you get the chance to complete one or more revision exercises to develop your skills and prepare you for your ECDL certification test. You should aim to complete the following steps without referring back to the previous lessons.

Manoeuvres

1. List the three main phases of any project.
2. Once a project is running, why would you need to make changes to a project plan?
3. What are "resources"?
4. What is a Gantt Chart?
5. Where can a project's start or end date be specified?
6. Where can additional project properties (such as the project's title and manager) be specified?
7. A new project will run 24 hours a day, 7 days a week. Where can this information be specified?

Sample answers can be found at the back of the guide.

*Now complete the **Record of Achievement Matrix** at the back of the guide. You should only move on when confident with the topics and features described in this section.*

Section 2 Project Files

By the end of this section you should be able to:

Save and close a project

Open a project

Switch between open projects

Work through the **Driving Lessons** in this section to gain an understanding of the above features.

For each **Driving Lesson**, read all of the **Park and Read** instructions and then, if applicable, perform the numbered steps of the **Manoeuvres**. Complete the **Revision** exercise(s) at the end of the section to test your knowledge.

Driving Lesson 10 - Saving a Project

Park and Read

To save a project so that you can open, edit and work with it later, you must save it. It is recommended that you save a project regularly to avoid losing information in the event of a software crash or power failure.

Manoeuvres

1. To save the current project, display the **FILE** tab.

*If you have not saved a project yet, both **Save** and **Save As** on the **FILE** tab will display the **Save As** screen (as the file has not yet been given a file name). If the project has already been saved, **Save** will immediately overwrite the original and the **Save As** screen will not appear.*

2. Click **Save** on the left panel. Then, select **Computer** and click the **Browse** button. The **Save As** dialog box is displayed.
3. Select the location where the data files for this guide are stored: within **Documents**, double click on **DATA FILES** followed by **ECDL** and finally **Project Planning**.
4. Enter the **File name** as **movie**.

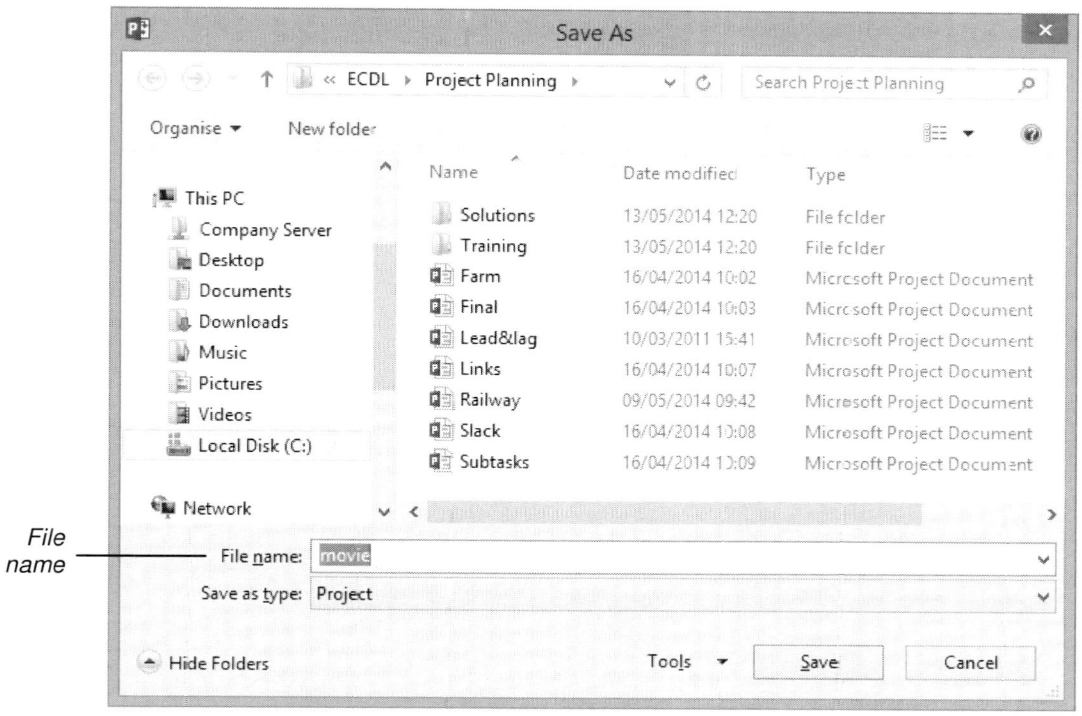

5. Click **Save** to save the project to the data folder. The **Title Bar** now shows the file name, **movie**.

Driving Lesson 11 - Closing a Project

Park and Read

When you are finished working with a project file, it needs to be closed. If any changes have been made to the project since it was last saved, you will be prompted to save again.

Manoeuvres

1. Before closing the project, let's first make a small change to it...
2. Click the **FILE** tab, FILE, to show the **Info** screen. Click **Project Information** on the right of the screen and then select **Advanced Properties** from the drop-down list.
3. On the **Summary** tab of the **Properties** dialog box, change the **Manager** name to **Monty Spangles**. Click **OK**.
4. Click **Close**. As a change has been made to the project, you will be prompted to save before closing.

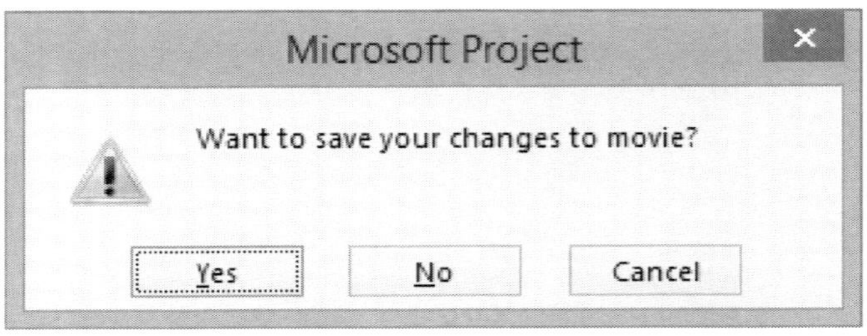

*This prompt will not appear unless changes have been made to the project after it was last saved. Clicking **Yes** will save changes and close the project; **No** will discard changes and close the project.*

5. For now, click **Cancel**. You will return to the **movie** project without closing it or saving/discarding changes.

*You can also close a project using the **Close Window** button, ☒, in the top right corner of the screen (the button below the program's **Close** button).*

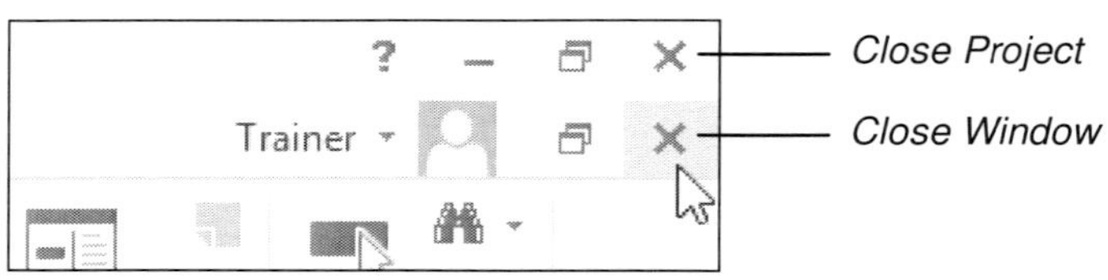

6. Click the **Close Window** button, ☒, as shown above (do not click the **Close** *Project* button as this will close *Project* as well as the open file).
7. A prompt to save changes appears again. This time click **Yes**. The project is saved and closed.

Driving Lesson 12 - Opening a Project

Park and Read

To read, edit and work with a saved project, you must first open it. If you used a project recently, you will find a quick link to it under **Recent Projects**. If not, the **Open** dialog box can be used to locate and open it instead.

Manoeuvres

1. *Project's* **New** screen should currently be displayed. Click **Open** on the left panel instead.

2. Locate the **Recent Projects** list on the right of the screen. This should show the last open file, **movie**, towards the top.

***.mpp** after the project's file name is the file's extension. This is used to inform* Windows *that the file is a* Microsoft Project *file. If you double click the file in Windows to open it, it will use this extension to start* Project.

3. Click **movie** once to open it. The project is displayed on-screen again.

4. Close the movie project.

5. Next, click the **FILE** tab again and select **Open**. This time, click **Computer** and then **Browse**. The **Open** dialog box appears.

6. Navigate to the location where the data files for this guide are stored.

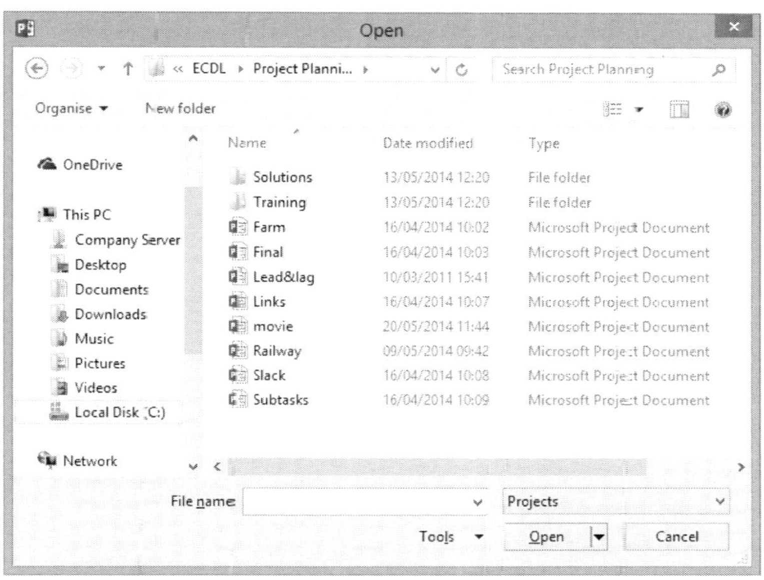

Driving Lesson 12 - Continued

*Notice that the **movie** project saved earlier now appears in this list.*

7. Select **Farm** and click **Open**. The project that opens was created to manage the summer crop season at a local farm.

*You can also open a project using the keyboard shortcut <**Ctrl O**>.*

8. Close the **Farm** project.

You will need to save, open and close projects throughout this guide.

*You can open more than one project at a time. You can then use the **Taskbar** to switch between them.*

*Want to create a new, blank project? Recall from lesson 2 that you can use the starting screen or **FILE** tab to create a new project at any time.*

Driving Lesson 13 - Revision

Park and Read

At the end of every section you get the chance to complete one or more revision exercises to develop your skills and prepare you for your ECDL certification test. You should aim to complete the following steps without referring back to the previous lessons.

Manoeuvres

1. You have been asked to set up a basic new project for a friend, *Fiona*. Use the **FILE** tab to create a new **Blank project**.
2. Set a **Start Date** for the project as **01/02/2017**.
3. Hide the **Timeline**.
4. Saturdays are normal working days on this project (08:00 to 12:00, 13:00 to 17:00). Change the project's working time to show this.
5. Place your mouse pointer over the dividing bar between the **Task List** and **Gantt Chart**. Drag the dividing bar so that **Duration** is the last column header visible before the **Gantt Chart** appears.
6. Open the **Properties** dialog box and, on the **Summary** tab, enter the **Subject** as **Fiona's Project Plan**.
7. Enter your own name as the **Author** and click **OK**.
8. Save the project as **basic plan** in the location where the data files for this guide are stored.
9. Close **basic plan** but leave *Project* open.
10. A sample project named **section2 revision complete** can be found in the **Revisions** folder within the data files folder. Open this now.
11. The project than opens is a model solution for the **basic plan** project that you have just created. You can compare your work against this.
12. Close *Project* and any open files (without saving any changes).
13. Open *Project* again and then open the **basic plan** project again.

On Project's *starting screen, you can click **Open Other Projects** on the left panel to display the **Open** screen.*

14. Finally, close *Project* again without saving changes to any open files.

Section 3
Tasks

By the end of this section you should be able to:

Identify and create tasks

Insert and remove tasks

Move tasks

Edit tasks

Assign durations to tasks

Understand milestones

Work through the **Driving Lessons** in this section to gain an understanding of the above features.

For each **Driving Lesson**, read all of the **Park and Read** instructions and then, if applicable, perform the numbered steps of the **Manoeuvres**. Complete the **Revision** exercise(s) at the end of the section to test your knowledge.

Driving Lesson 14 - Identifying Tasks

Park and Read

One of *Microsoft Project's* most useful features is its ability to effectively represent project activities as virtual **tasks**. Unlike in paper-based plans, these tasks can be easily edited and rearranged to help create the most efficient project design possible.

*A **task** in* Project *is any activity that needs to be accomplished within a specific period of time.*

Before adding detail to your project plan, it helps to define the broad goals of the project first – what is it that you hope to achieve and how will you accomplish it? These high-level goals will help you to identify the key tasks that need to be performed to achieve the results you are after.

For instance, to make a movie, the following goals would need to be achieved:

- Write script
- Raise finance
- Find location
- Employ people
- Prepare filming
- Shoot movie
- Release movie

These goals can now be turned into high-level tasks in your project plan. Of course, they are obviously not detailed enough to be of much use, but they do give an overview of the main stages of the project – an ideal starting point for any project plan.

All tasks should produce a deliverable (e.g. a script or a movie) or have a means of measuring the percentage of work completed during its progress (e.g. 50% of the movie has been filmed so far).

Once the main goals of the project have been worked out, they can then be broken down further into more manageable "subtasks", as you will see later.

*Breaking your project down into smaller chunks of work is an important first step when creating a project plan. Professionals often refer to the resulting list of tasks as a **Work Breakdown Structure** (**WBS**).*

Driving Lesson 15 - Adding Tasks

Park and Read

Tasks entered into *Project* can be **Manually Scheduled** or **Auto Scheduled**. This guide will only create automatically scheduled tasks as they are more useful and easier for beginners to work with.

As you will see later, one of the most powerful features of Project *is its ability to automatically reschedule tasks when a change occurs. For example, if you change a task's duration,* Project *will automatically update all of the other relevant tasks that come after it and change the project's end date for you.*

Manually scheduled tasks are static and never change unless specifically updated. These can be difficult and time-consuming to work with but give advanced users more control over their plans.

Manoeuvres

1. Start *Project*.
2. Open the **movie** project created earlier.

*An up-to-date model copy of the **movie** project is available in the data files folder **Training**. This is named **section3 movie**. If you would like to use this, open the project and save it as **movie** in the main data files folder.*

3. Examine the **Status Bar**. Notice that **NEW TASKS** are currently **MANUALLY SCHEDULED**.

4. Click on **NEW TASKS: MANUALLY SCHEDULED** on the **Status Bar** and select **Auto Scheduled** instead. *Project* will now automatically schedule tasks in relation to each other.

*Tasks are typed into the **Task Name** column in the **Task List**. They should ideally be entered in the order you want them to occur during the project.*

5. Click once in the first row of the **Task Name** column to select it.

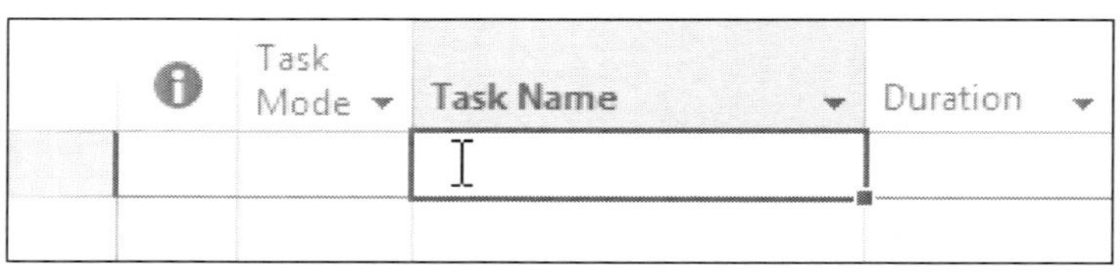

Driving Lesson 15 - Continued

6. Enter **Write a script** and press <**Enter**> to complete the entry and move to the next row.

		Task Mode	Task Name	Duration
1			Write a script	1 day?

*Note that the duration is entered as **1 day?** in the **Duration** column.*

7. Next, add the following tasks, each on a new row:

   Employ people
   Prepare filming
   Shoot movie
   Release movie

8. Your project plan should now feature 5 different tasks, as shown below.

		Task Mode	Task Name	Duration
1			Write a script	1 day?
2			Employ people	1 day?
3			Prepare filming	1 day?
4			Shoot movie	1 day?
5			Release movie	1 day?

9. Save the **movie** project and leave it open for the next lesson.

Driving Lesson 16 - Inserting or Deleting Tasks

Park and Read

As you learned in the previous lesson, new tasks are easily added to the bottom of the **Task List**. However, you may also want to insert new tasks between others or remove unwanted tasks completely.

Manoeuvres

1. Your project plan currently contains 5 tasks. Let's add some more...
2. In the **Task List**, click <u>once</u> on the **Shoot movie** task name to select it.
3. Then, press the <**Insert**> key on your keyboard to insert a new row.

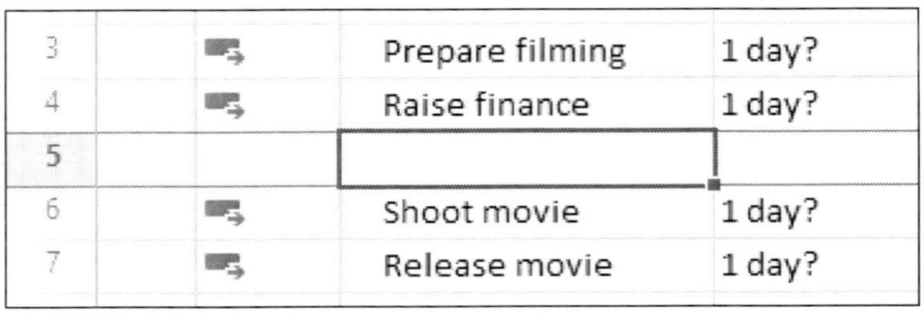

4. Enter the new task **Raise finance** and press <**Enter**>.
5. Let's try another way to add tasks. With the **Shoot movie** task still selected, click the **Insert Task** button in the **Insert** group (click the button's icon, not the drop-down arrow).

6. Type **Find location** to overwrite **<New Task>** and press <**Enter**>.
7. These two new tasks replace **Prepare filming**. Place the mouse pointer over the **3** on the **Row Heading Bar**. The pointer changes to →.

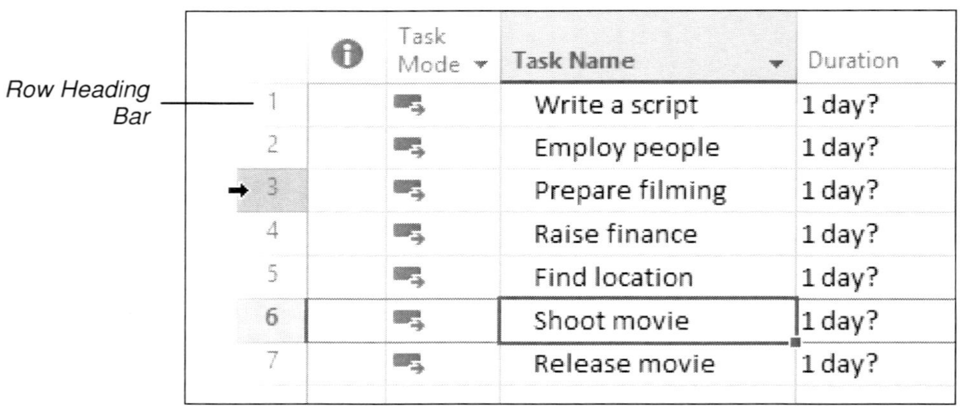

8. Click once to select the entire row and then press <**Delete**> to remove it.

*You can also right click a task and select **Delete Task** to remove it.*

Driving Lesson 17 - Moving or Copying Tasks

Park and Read

It is simple to move tasks up and down in the **Task List**, or create a copy of a task that can be edited independently from the original.

Manoeuvres

1. The **Raise finance** task is currently in the wrong location and should come *before* **Employ people**.
2. Move your mouse pointer over **3** on the **Row Heading Bar** and click once to select this row.
3. The cursor changes to a four-way arrow, . Click and drag the task row number upwards to a new position between rows **1** and **2** (a grey "T line" appears to show where the moved task will be inserted).

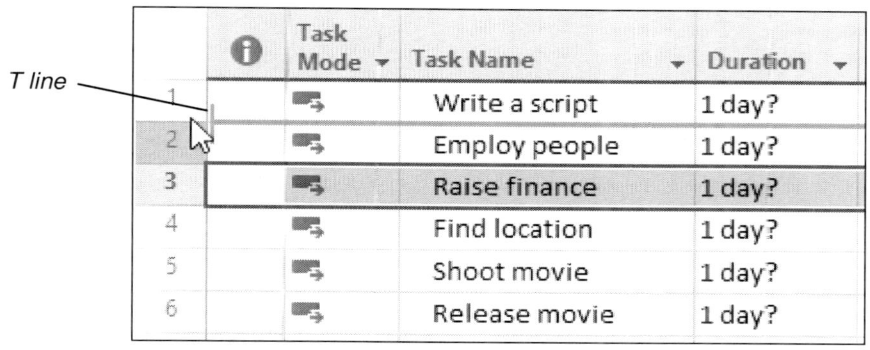

The T line shows where the selected task will be inserted when dropped

4. Release the mouse button to drop the **Raise finance** row. **Raise finance** should now be task **2**.
5. Select the row for task **3**, **Employ people**, using the **Row Heading Bar**.
6. Someone needs to be hired to write the script. Click **Copy**, , in the **Clipboard** group. The selected task is copied.
7. Select the row for task **1**, **Write a script**, using the **Row Heading Bar**.

8. Click **Paste** (click the button's icon, not its drop-down arrow).
9. The copied task is pasted into the **Task List** and appears at the location of the previously selected row (all rows are moved down one to accommodate it). You will edit the copied task name in the next lesson.

Copying a task allows you to duplicate a task's information, including start dates and durations (which you will learn more about later). If you do not need this information, however, it is often easier to simply insert a new task.

Driving Lesson 18 - Editing Task Names

Park and Read

A task name can be replaced by simply selecting it and then overtyping. Alternatively, you can change a name using standard text editing techniques.

Task changes can be immediately "undone" using the ***Undo*** *button, , on the* ***Quick Access Toolbar****. The drop down arrow on the right of the button allows a sequence of tasks to be undone at the same time.*

Manoeuvres

1. Click once on the task name **Employ People** on row **1** (not row 4). Type **Find a story** to overtype and replace this text. Press <**Enter**> to confirm the change.

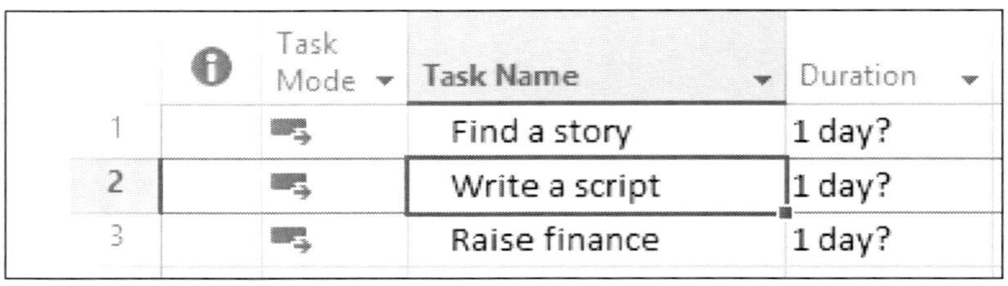

		Task Mode	Task Name	Duration
1			Find a story	1 day?
2			Write a script	1 day?
3			Raise finance	1 day?

2. You've decided that it will take far too long to research a story for the film – it would be much easier to hire somebody else to write the script. Click the **Find a story** task name once to select it again.

3. Notice the mouse pointer changes to I when over text.

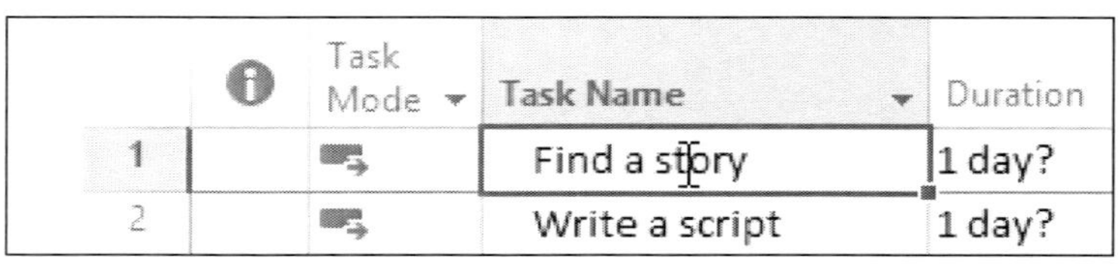

		Task Mode	Task Name	Duration
1			Find a story	1 day?
2			Write a script	1 day?

4. Click to place the cursor in the name text and then, using the cursor (arrow) and <**Backspace**>/<**Delete**> keys, change the text to **Find a writer**. Press <**Enter**> to confirm the change.

5. Next, select the task name **Release movie**. Then, using whichever technique you prefer, change this to **Promote movie** and press <**Enter**>.

6. The last change was a mistake. Click the **Undo** button, , to reverse the last action. **Release movie** reappears in task **7**.

*A change can be cancelled by pressing <****Esc****> before completing the change.*

Next to ***Undo*** *is the* ***Redo*** *button, . This button undoes the actions performed using* ***Undo****.*

Driving Lesson 19 - Task Durations

Park and Read

All tasks take a certain amount of time to complete. This time is known as the **duration** and can be entered in:

- **Months (mo)**
- **Weeks (w)**
- **Days (d)**
- **Hours (h)**
- **Minutes (m)**

*Days (**d**) are the default unit of time measurement in* Project. *However, the abbreviations above (e.g. **mo**, **w**, **h** and **m**) can be used to specify a different unit of measurement.*

If a task's duration is **estimated**, it appears with a question mark, **?**, after the duration. However, as most task durations can be considered estimates at the planning stage, this feature is rarely needed.

Estimated durations are best used by advanced, experienced project planners who need to distinguish between accurate estimates and rough guesses.

Manoeuvres

1. Examine the **Duration** column in the **Task List**. When new tasks are **Auto Scheduled**, they are given a default estimated **Duration** of **1 day?**

*Notice that the **Gantt Chart** displays task durations as bars, (all starting on the start date of the project). Watch these change during this lesson.*

2. Let's change the durations of the tasks in the project plan. First, click <u>once</u> on the **Duration** for task **1** to select it.

		Task Mode	Task Name	Duration
1			Find a writer	1 day?
2			Write a script	1 day?

3. Type **2** and press <**Enter**>. As the default unit of time measurement in *Project* is days, the **Duration** for task **1** is now **2 days**.

		Task Mode	Task Name	Duration
1			Find a writer	2 days

Driving Lesson 19 - Continued

*Notice that the duration of task **1** also increases on the **Gantt Chart**.*

When adjusting a selected duration, the up/down spinners, , can be used to increase or decrease the current value.

4. Change the **Duration** for task **2** to **2** days also.
5. Change the **Duration** for task **3** to 1 week. To do this, type **1w** and press <**Enter**>.

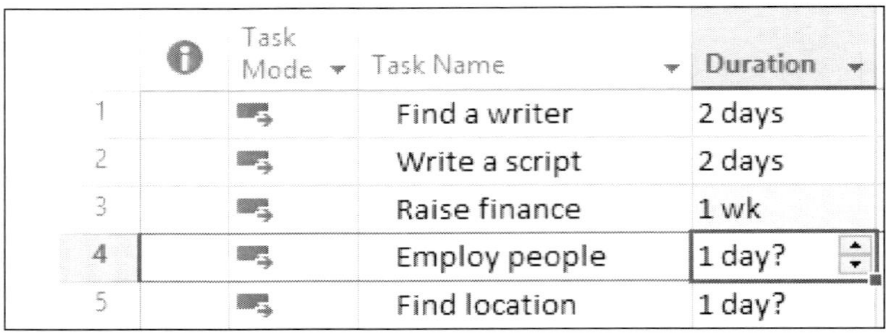

Recall that the abbreviations at the start of this lesson can be used to specify different units of time measurement (e.g. weeks, months, hours).

6. Add the following **Durations** to the remaining tasks:

Employ people	**3 days**
Find location	**6 days**
Shoot movie	**3 weeks**
Release movie	**4 hours**

*Notice that the durations are no longer shown as estimated, **?**.*

*Remember, Sunday has been specified as a non-working day. Any tasks spanning a weekend, e.g. **Find location**, will not count Sunday.*

7. It will take much longer to write the script than 2 days. Change the duration of task **2** to **2 weeks**.

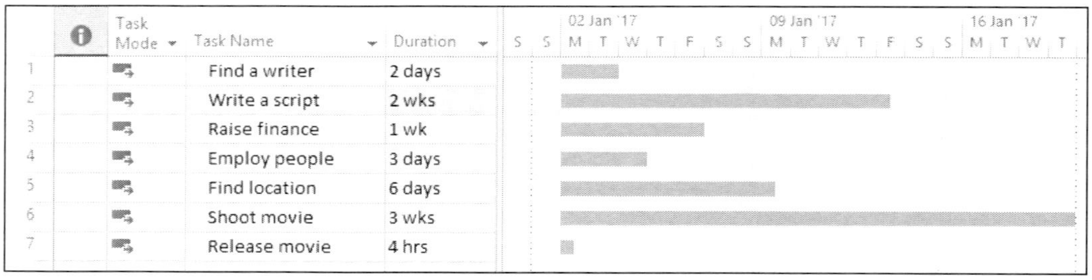

For a project schedule to be accurate, effective and of maximum value, the times (durations) allocated to tasks should be as realistic as possible.

Driving Lesson 20 - Splitting Tasks

Park and Read

The duration of a task in *Project* represents the time it will take to complete that task, from start to end, without breaks. However, if you need to interrupt a task (perhaps because it can't be completed all in one go), you can **split** it.

Manoeuvres

1. Select task **5**, **Find location** in the **Task List**.

*To select a task, simply click its **Task Name** in the **Task List** once.*

2. There will be a lot of travelling involved in finding a location to shoot the movie and you really don't want to spend six days back-to-back doing this. It would be much better to perform the task in three separate stages with a number of "days off" in-between. Let's split the task...

3. Click **Split Task**, , in the **Schedule** group. Notice the large **ToolTip** that appears.

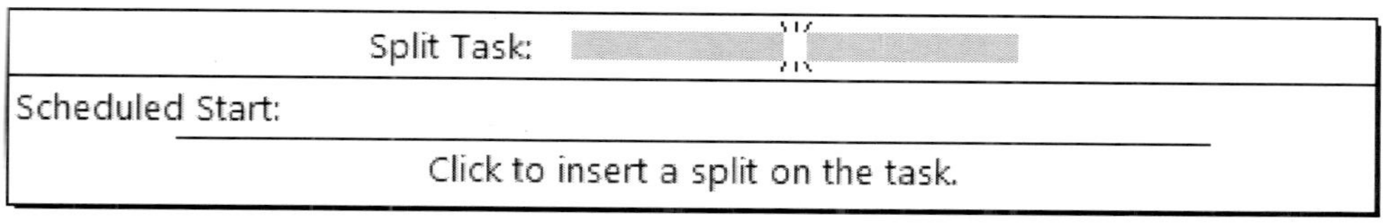

4. On the **Gantt Chart**, move your mouse pointer over the bar for task **5**. The pointer changes to .

5. Using the **Timescale** for reference, place the mouse pointer over the *first Wednesday* for task **5** (i.e. the third day of the task). Notice that the ToolTip's **Scheduled Start** shows when the split will occur.

Timescale

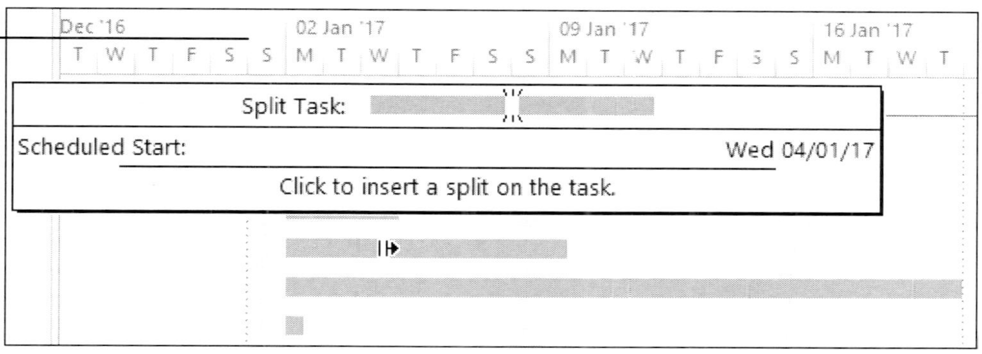

6. Click once to split the task into two parts. The split appears as a sequence of dots (the task is suspended where the dots appear).

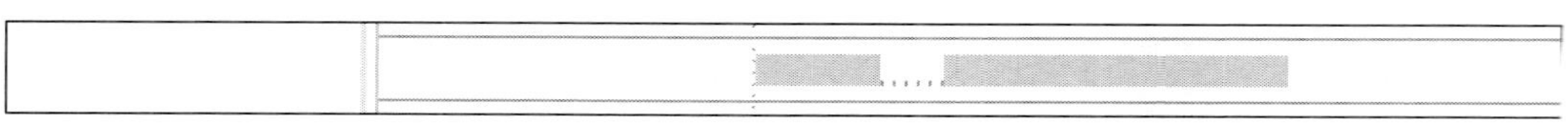

Driving Lesson 20 - Continued

7. Next, place your mouse pointer over the second part of the bar. The pointer changes to ✥. Click and drag the second part of the bar so that it starts on the *first Monday of the week after* (09/01/17)

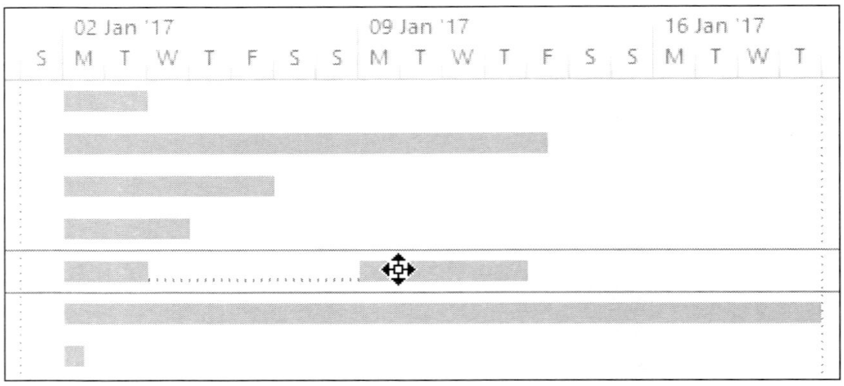

8. Notice that the dotted line is extended. The task runs for two days, is suspended until the following Monday, and then resumes.

9. Click **Split Task**, , again. This time, place the mouse pointer over the *second Wednesday in January* for task **5** (11/01/17).

You can click and drag at the same time to create and adjust a split's duration.

10. Click and drag the second part of the bar so that it starts on the *first Monday of the following week.*

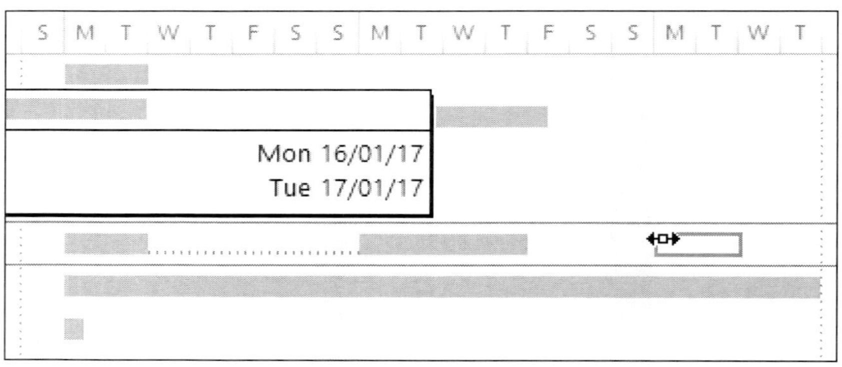

11. Task **5** is now divided into three stages.

12. Next, split task **1**, **Find a writer**, into two. The task should run for one day, be suspended for three days, and then run again for one day.

13. The previous change was made in error. Click and drag the second part of task **1** to the left so that it reconnects with the first part again. The split is removed.

Driving Lesson 21 - Milestones

Park and Read

Milestones are used to mark the start or end of important events in the life of a project. For example, milestones can mark the achievement of a significant goal or the start or end of a particular phase.

Milestones are simply tasks with zero duration. Any task can be made into a milestone by changing its duration to **0 days**. Milestones appear as a black diamond with the date that they are scheduled to occur.

Manoeuvres

1. Select task **1**, **Find a writer**, and press <**Insert**> to insert a new task.
2. Name the new task **Make a movie**.
3. On the first blank row beneath **Release movie**, add the new task **Movie complete**. These milestones represent the start and end of the project.
4. Change the duration of both tasks to **0 days**.

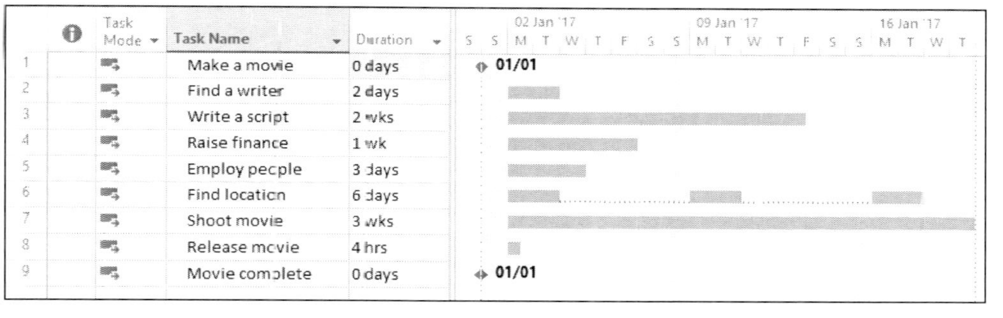

	Task Mode	Task Name	Duration	Gantt
1		Make a movie	0 days	01/01
2		Find a writer	2 days	
3		Write a script	2 wks	
4		Raise finance	1 wk	
5		Employ people	3 days	
6		Find location	6 days	
7		Shoot movie	3 wks	
8		Release movie	4 hrs	
9		Movie complete	0 days	01/01

*Notice the milestone icons, ◆, on the **Gantt Chart**.*

5. Next, add a new milestone named **Start filming** <u>above</u> task **7**, **Shoot movie**. This is an important date in the movie's project plan.

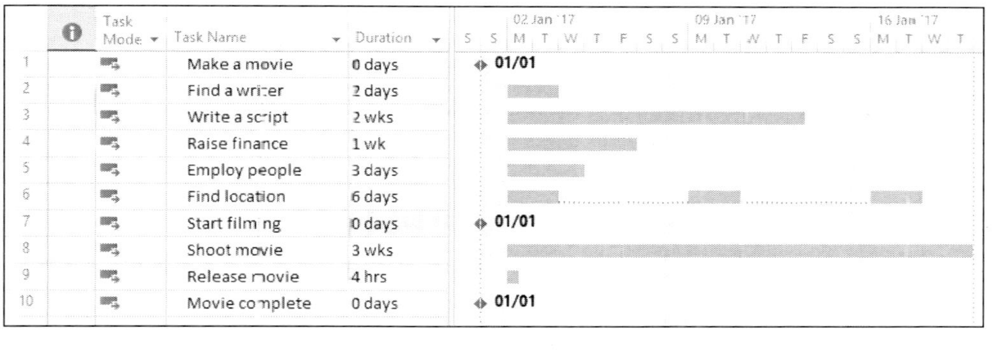

	Task Mode	Task Name	Duration	Gantt
1		Make a movie	0 days	01/01
2		Find a writer	2 days	
3		Write a script	2 wks	
4		Raise finance	1 wk	
5		Employ people	3 days	
6		Find location	6 days	
7		Start filming	0 days	01/01
8		Shoot movie	3 wks	
9		Release movie	4 hrs	
10		Movie complete	0 days	01/01

All tasks and milestones currently start together on day 1 of the project. This doesn't make much sense at the moment, but you will change their dates and build a more useful schedule later.

Driving Lesson 22 - Notes

Park and Read

Notes can be attached to tasks in *Project*. This allows you to add a little more detail beyond what is shown on the **Task List** and **Gantt Chart**.

Manoeuvres

1. Select task **6**, **Find location**.
2. From the **Properties** group on the **TASK** tab, click **Task Notes**, . The **Task Information** dialog box appears with the **Notes** tab selected.
3. In the text area below **Notes**, enter the text **Location must be within 20 miles of studio**.

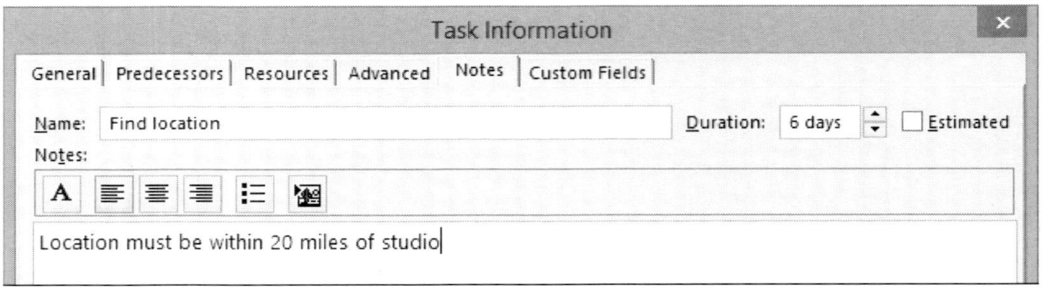

4. Click **OK**. Notice that an icon, , appears in the **Indicators** column to show there is a note for this task. Move the mouse over the icon to see it.

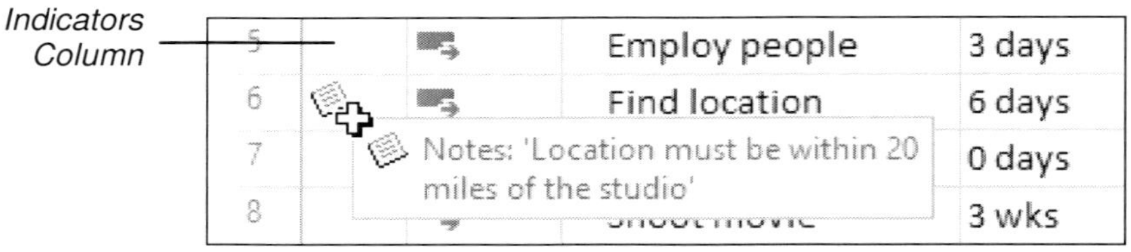

*The **Indicators** column, , in the **Task List** is used to highlight important task information. You will see more icons added to this column later.*

5. Add the following note to task **2**, **Find a writer**: **Writer must be a famous author - maybe Joe King Rowling?**
6. Add the following note to milestone **10**, **Movie complete**: **Wrap party to be held at the Hotel Casablanca**.
7. 20 miles doesn't give you much scope to find a good location to shoot the movie. Double click on the note icon for task **6**, **Find location**. Edit the note to **Location must be within 300 miles of studio** and click **OK**.
8. The note that you added to task **2**, **Find a writer**, is maybe a little too optimistic! Edit and delete the note text. The note icon is removed.

Driving Lesson 23 - Hyperlinks

Park and Read

You can add a **hyperlink** to a task which will link to another file, web page or e-mail address.

Manoeuvres

1. Insert a new task <u>above</u> task **9**, **Release movie**. Enter the task name **Review budget** and set its **Duration** to **2 hours**.

8			Shoot movie	3 wks
9			Review budget	2 hrs
10			Release movie	4 hrs
11			Movie complete	0 days

2. Right click on the new task **9**, **Review budget**. From the bottom of the pop-up menu that appears, select **Hyperlink**, Hyperlink... .

3. A hyperlink is to be created to a spreadsheet containing budget information. Make sure **Existing File or Web Page** is selected at the left of the **Insert Hyperlink** dialog box.

Notice that you can also create hyperlinks to other places in the current project, to a new blank file, or to an e-mail address.

4. The **Documents** folder should be selected in **Look in**. Below this, double click on **DATA FILES**, then **ECDL**, then **Project Planning** to display the files for this guide. Click the *Excel* file **Budget** once to select it.

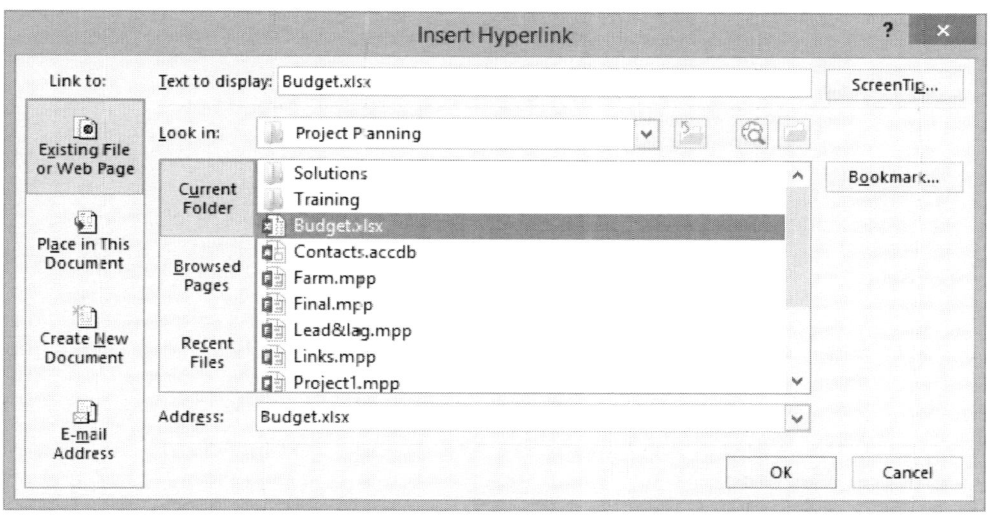

5. Click **OK** to create the hyperlink. Notice the hyperlink icon, , that appears in the **Indicators** column.

Driving Lesson 23 - Continued

6. Move the mouse pointer over the hyperlink symbol. It changes to a pointing hand.

7. Click once to follow the hyperlink. A security notice may appear – click **Yes** to continue if it does.

8. *Excel* starts and opens the **Budget** workbook. Close *Excel*.

9. Next, attach a hyperlink to task **2**, **Find a writer**. Make sure **Existing File or Web Page** is selected at the left of the **Insert Hyperlink** dialog box.

10. A friend has recommended *CiA Training* to write the movie. Let's create a link to their webpage. Enter **www.ciatraining.co.uk** in the **Address** box.

11. Click **OK**. Try the new hyperlink: it opens in your computer's default Internet browser.

12. Close the Internet browser and return to *Project*.

13. Your friend has provided a *Word* document with a list of authors to consider instead. Right click on the hyperlink icon for task **2**, **Find a writer** and select **Hyperlink | Edit Hyperlink**.

14. In the dialog box, select **Existing File or Web Page** and navigate to the data folder. Select the document **Contacts.docx** and click **OK**.

15. The hyperlink now links to the contact file; check it and then close *Word*.

16. None of these contacts are suitable. Right click on the hyperlink icon for task **2**, **Find a writer** and select **Hyperlink | Clear Hyperlinks**. The hyperlink is deleted.

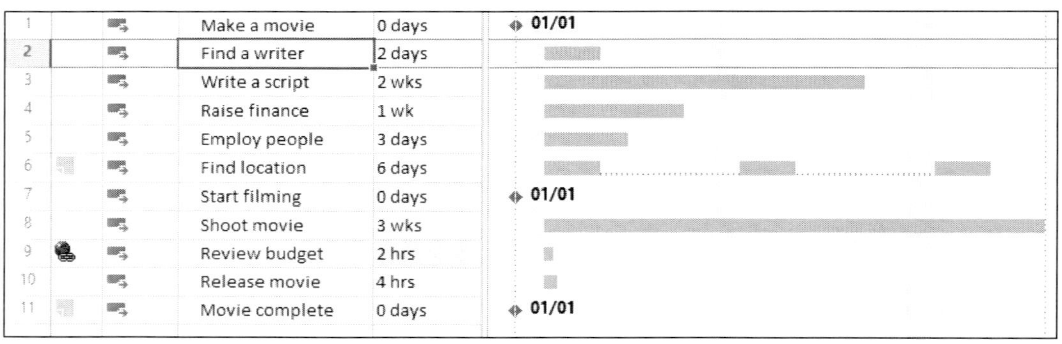

*Alternatively, click **Clear** in the **Editing** group,* Clear, *and select **Clear Hyperlinks**.*

17. Save the **movie** project and close it, but leave *Project* open.

Driving Lesson 24 - Revision

Park and Read

At the end of every section you get the chance to complete one or more revision exercises to develop your skills and prepare you for your ECDL certification test. You should aim to complete the following steps without referring back to the previous lessons.

Manoeuvres

1. In *Project*, what is a **task**?
2. If you want *Project's* powerful scheduling features to organise tasks for you, should you use manual or automatic scheduling?
3. What is a task's **duration**?
4. New auto-scheduled tasks appear with a duration of **1 day?** What does the question mark indicate?
5. Which keyboard shortcut can be used to add a new task above the currently selected task?
6. How do you delete a task from the **Task List**?
7. How can tasks be rearranged in the **Task List**?
8. How do you edit a task's name?
9. If you want a task to be interrupted for a time, what feature can you use?
10. What is a **milestone**?
11. Why might you want to add a note to a task?
12. Why might you want to add a hyperlink to a task?

Now complete the ***Record of Achievement Matrix*** *at the back of the guide. You should only move on when confident with the topics and features described in this section.*

Section 4
File Formats & Templates

By the end of this section you should be able to:

Save a project in a different file format

Create a project template

Use a project template

Work through the **Driving Lessons** in this section to gain an understanding of the above features.

For each **Driving Lesson**, read all of the **Park and Read** instructions and then, if applicable, perform the numbered steps of the **Manoeuvres**. Complete the **Revision** exercise(s) at the end of the section to test your knowledge.

Driving Lesson 25 - Saving with a New Name

Park and Read

You can save an open project with a different file name and then work on the new file without affecting the original.

This feature is useful if you want to create a new project based on the contents of another.

Manoeuvres

1. Open the **movie** project created earlier.

*An up-to-date model copy of the **movie** project is available in the data files folder **Training**. This is named **section4 movie**. If you would like to use this, open the project and save it as **movie** in the main data files folder.*

2. Display the **FILE** tab and select **Save As**.
3. With **Computer** selected, click the recently used data files folder **Project Planning** below **Recent Folders**. The **Save As** dialog box appears.

*If the **Project Planning** folder does not appear below **Recent Folders**, click the **Browse** button and navigate to it.*

4. Change the **File name** at the bottom of the dialog box to **tv show**.
5. Click **Save** to save the project as a new file. Notice that the new file name appears on the **Title Bar**.
6. You can now edit this project without affecting the original **movie** project. On the **TASK** tab, click the drop-down arrow on the **Find** button, , in the **Editing** group.

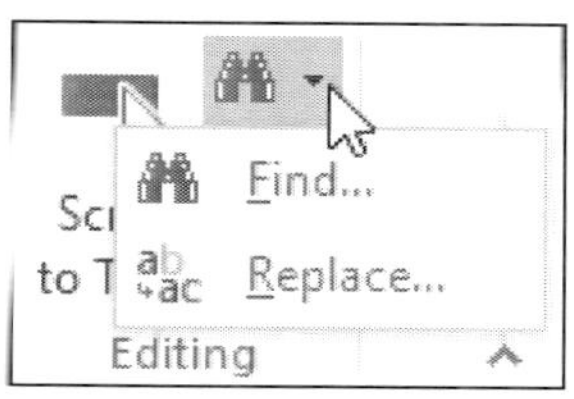

7. Select **Replace** to show the **Replace** dialog box. This feature allows you to quickly search for and replace text in your project.
8. Enter **movie** in the **Find what** box.
9. Enter **tv show** in the **Replace with** box.
10. Select **All Visible** to search the entire project.

Driving Lesson 25 - Continued

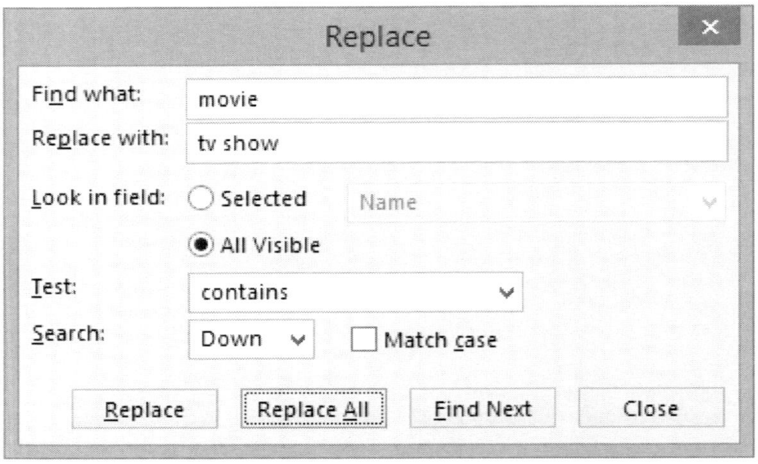

Find Next *and* ***Replace*** *allow you to step through each search result one at a time, making or skipping changes.*

11. Click **Replace All**.

12. Click **OK** to acknowledge the number of changes made. Click **Close** and notice the change: all instances of the word **movie** have been replaced by **tv show**.
13. Display the **FILE** tab and select **Save** to save the project using the same file name (**tv show**).

To quickly save a project using the same file name, click the ***Save*** *button, on the* ***Quick Access Toolbar****. Alternatively, press <****Ctrl S****>.*

14. Close the project.
15. Next, open the **movie** project again. Notice that the changes to **tv show** have not affected this project.
16. Leave the **movie** project open for the next lesson.

You can also use the ***Find*** *button in the* ***Editing*** *group to search for text without replacing it. To do this, select* ***Find*** *from the* ***Find*** *button's drop-down menu (or simply click the button's icon rather than its drop-down arrow).*

Driving Lesson 26 - Exporting a Project

Park and Read

A project can be saved in various different formats so that it can be used elsewhere. Files such as spreadsheets, text files (plain, CSV and XML) and even PDF documents can all be created.

Manoeuvres

1. With the project **movie** open, display the **FILE** tab and select **Save As**.
2. With **Computer** selected, click the recently used data files folder **Project Planning** below **Recent Folders**.

*If the **Project Planning** folder does not appear below **Recent Folders**, click the **Browse** button and navigate to it.*

3. To see the various formats in which the current project can be saved, click the **Save as type** drop-down button at the bottom of the dialog box.

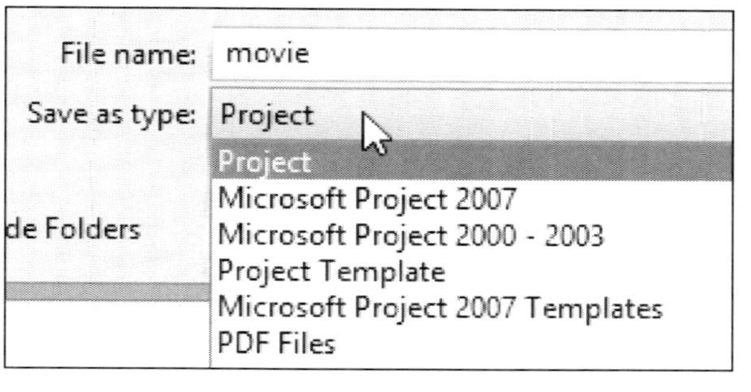

4. From the list of file types displayed, select **Excel Workbook** to save the project as a spreadsheet.
5. Change the **File name** to **movie spreadsheet**. Click **Save**.
6. The *Project* **Export Wizard** starts. Read the text on the first screen and then click **Next**.
7. Choose **Selected Data** and click **Next**.

*Mapping is used to convert project data into other formats. For example, the **Start Date** or **Duration** columns in* Project *can be converted into similar columns in* Excel.

8. Select **New map** and click **Next**. Select to export **Tasks** only and make sure **Export includes headers** is checked. Click **Next**.
9. Click once on **(Click here to map a field)** and then click the small drop-down arrow, ⌄, that appears to the right of the box.

Driving Lesson 26 - Continued

10. Examine the field types available. Then select **Name**.

11. On the row below, select a field type of **Scheduled Duration**. Edit the field name in the **To: Excel Field** column to **Duration**.

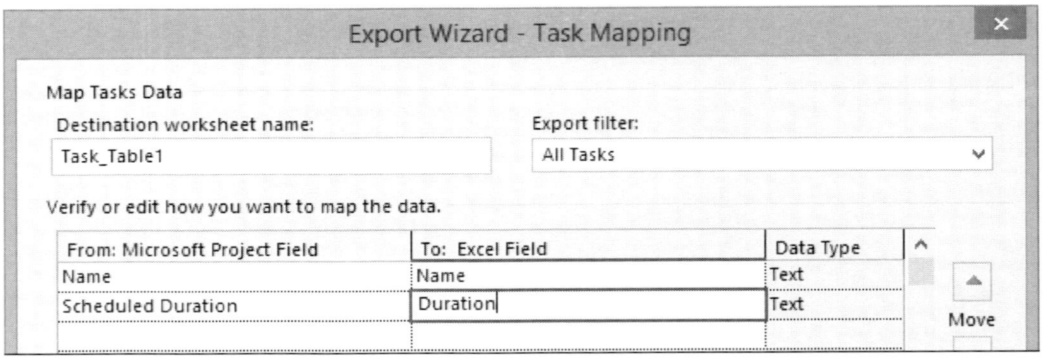

12. Notice the **Data Type** properties. These can be edited, but for now click **Finish**. The project is saved as a spreadsheet.

13. Display the **FILE** tab and select **Save As** again. This time save the project in the data files folder as a **PDF File** named **movie pdf**.

14. At the **Document Export Options** dialog box, leave the settings as they are and click **Ok**. The project is saved as a PDF file.

PDF files are print-ready copies of a document that can be easily sent to other people via e-mail or the Internet. Users cannot edit a PDF file and they do not need Project *in order to open, view and print its contents.*

15. Finally, display the **FILE** tab and select **Save As** again. This time save the project in the data files folder as an **XML Format** file named **movie xml**.

The XML file format can be used to exchange data between programs. It is not designed to be read by users in its raw format.

16. Close the **movie** file and then close *Project.*

17. Next, click the **File Explorer** or **Windows Explorer** button, , on the **Taskbar** and navigate to the data file folder. The three files created in this lesson will appear in the list of files.

18. Try opening each of the new files. Examine their content, and then close the program that opened them.

19. Close all open programs and windows and return to the **Desktop**.

Driving Lesson 27 - Creating a Template

Park and Read

To save you time, a **template** can be used as the basis for a new project. A template is simply a project file that has been saved in a special templates folder to be used as a starting point for other project plans.

Manoeuvres

1. Start *Project*. On the starting screen that appears, select **Blank Project** to create a new project based on the default, blank template.

*A new project can be started at any time using the **New** screen on the **FILE** tab.*

2. As you now know, all new tasks are **Manually Scheduled** by default. Select **NEW TASKS: AUTO SCHEDULED** on the **Status Bar** instead.
3. Display the **FILE** tab and, on the **Info** screen, click the **Project Information** drop-down and select **Advanced Properties**.
4. In the **Subject** box, enter **A project created using my new template**.
5. Enter your name as **Author** and **Manager**, and **CiA Training** as **Company**.

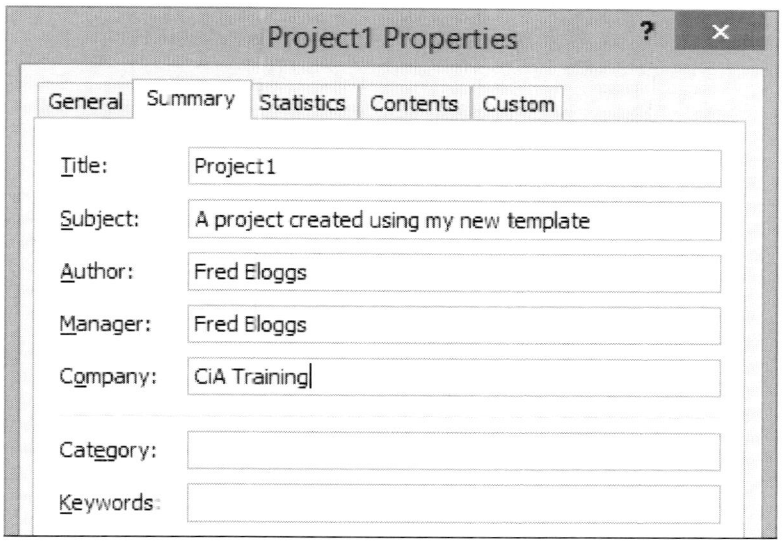

6. Click **OK**.

You do not need to set a start date for a template; this is selected when you create a new project based on it.

7. Click the **Back** button, , to return to the new blank project.

Driving Lesson 27 - Continued

8. Enter a new task on row **1** named **My Project Start**. Make it a milestone by setting its duration to **0 days**.

9. Enter a second task on row **2** named **My Project Finish**. Make it a milestone also.

10. Insert a new row <u>above</u> task **2**. Enter the name **First Task Goes Here**.

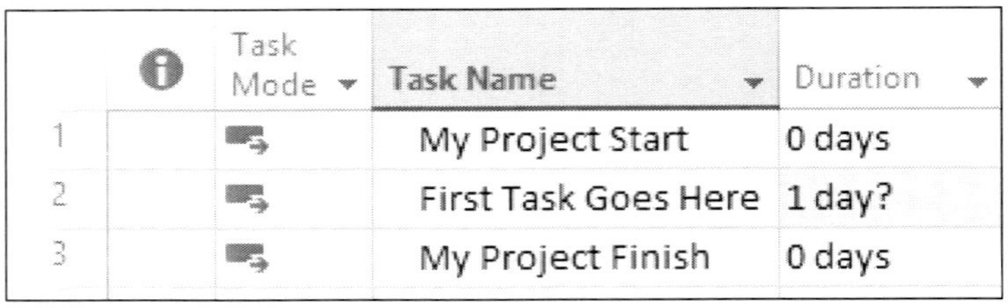

11. Using the **VIEW** tab, make sure the **Timeline** is hidden.

12. Finally, drag the dividing bar between the **Task List** and **Gantt Chart** so that **Duration** is the last column shown in the **Task List**.

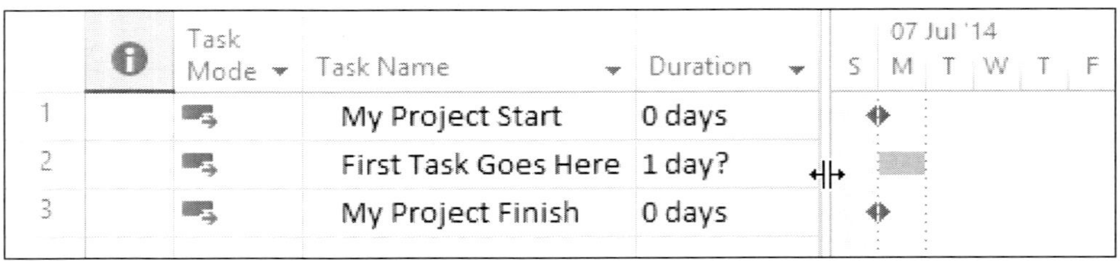

You've now set this project up just as you like it: auto-scheduling is selected, project properties and project information have been set, and a few starting tasks have been created.

13. Leave the project open for the next lesson.

Driving Lesson 28 - Saving a Template

Park and Read

Before you can use a custom template, you first need to save it to a special templates folder on your computer. *Project* will display the contents of this folder on the **New** screen.

When you first create a template, you may need to select a personal templates folder to save it in. All new templates will then be saved here automatically.

Manoeuvres

1. Display the **FILE** tab and select **Options** to display the **Project Options** dialog box. You can use the settings available here to change default options and customise how *Project* works.

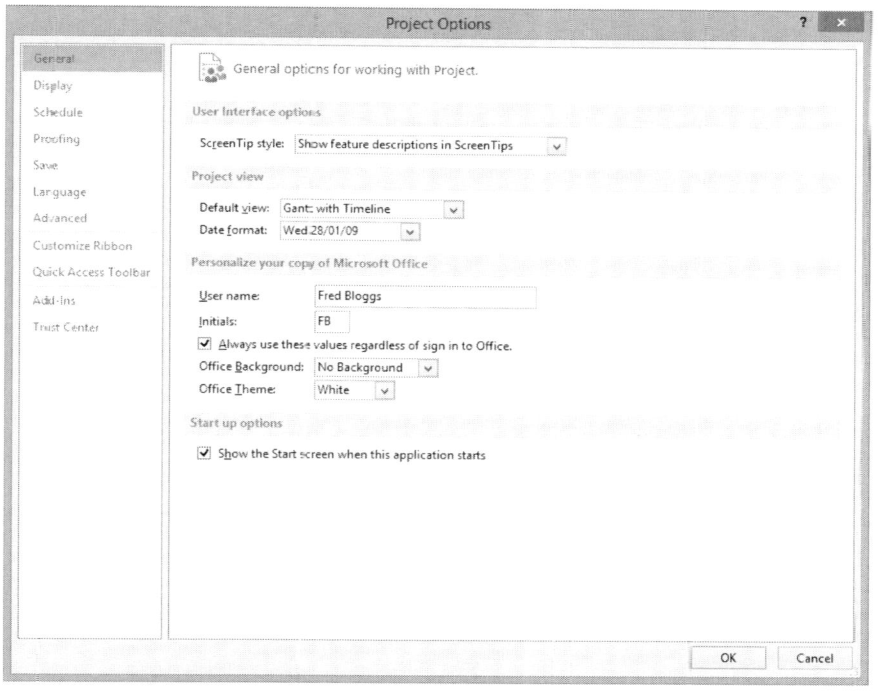

2. Select **Save** on the left of the dialog box to display a range of file saving options on the right. Locate the **Save templates** group.
3. Click **Browse** to the right of **Default personal templates location**. In the **Modify Location** dialog box, navigate to the data files folder for this guide. Select the folder **My Templates** and click **OK**.
4. Notice the path that appears in the **Default personal templates location**.

Driving Lesson 28 - Continued

5. Click **OK** to save these settings.

You only need to set a personal templates folder location once. From now on, all templates can be saved and opened from here.

6. The project that you created in the previous lesson should be on-screen. Let's save this as a template so it can be used as a starting point for other future projects. Display the **FILE** tab and select **Save As**.

7. With **Computer** selected, click the **Browse** button.

8. Next, click the **Save as type** drop-down button at the bottom of the dialog box. From the file types that appear, select **Project Template**. Notice that the location jumps to the **My Templates** folder.

9. Change the **File name** to **My Project Template** and click **Save**. Read the prompt that appears and select all five of the checkboxes.

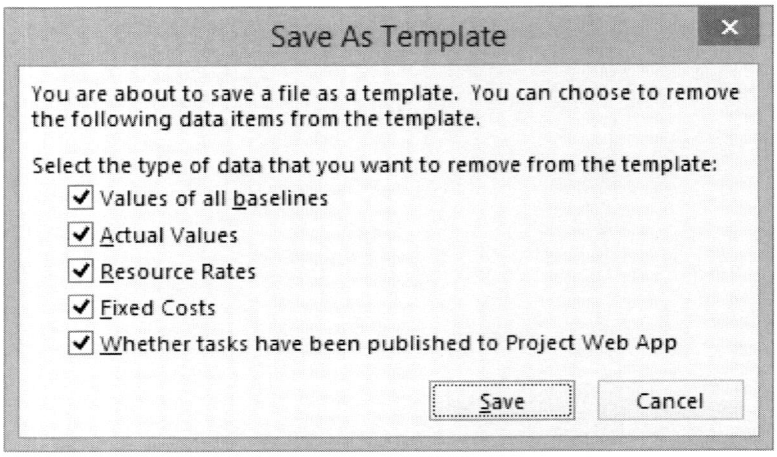

You do not want any progress information to be saved in a template as this may cause problems for other future projects based upon it.

10. Click **Save**. The project has now been saved as a template.

*Normal project files have a **.mpp** file extension. Template files, however, have a **.mpt** file extension.*

11. Close the project – you will create a new project based on this template in the next lesson.

Driving Lesson 29 - Using a Template

Park and Read

Once you have created a template, you can use it as the basis for new projects. All of the information created in the template will appear by default (and no changes to the new project will affect the template).

There are also many templates available online to help you create different types of project. These are available on Project's ***New*** *screen.*

Manoeuvres

1. The **New** screen is currently displayed. Scroll down to see some of the various online templates available.
2. Back at the top of the screen, select **PERSONAL** (found just above **Blank Project**). The contents of the **My Templates** folder are displayed.
3. Click once on **My Project Template**. On the dialog box that appears, select a **Start Date** of the *first Monday of next month*.

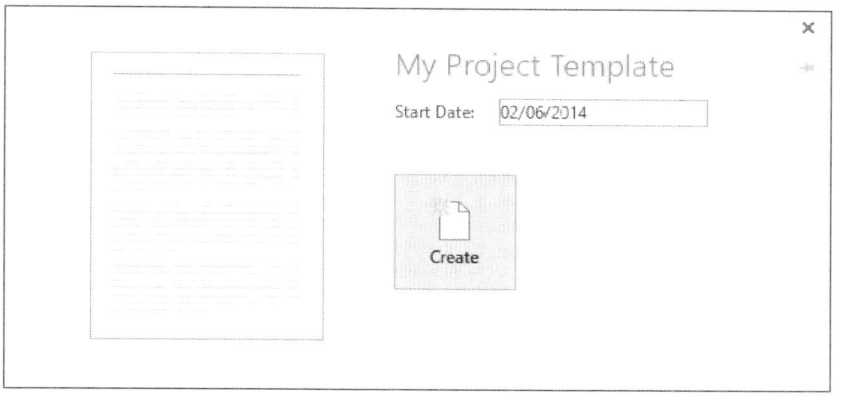

4. Click **Create** to start a new project based upon the **My Project Template**. Notice that the new auto-scheduled project starts on the date selected.
5. Change the **Task Name** for task **2** to **Create widgets** and set a **Duration** of **1 week**.
6. Display the **FILE** tab and click **Save**. As this is a new, unsaved project, the **Save As** screen appears (**Save** will not replace the original template).
7. Save the new project in the data files folder with the name **widgets**. Close the project.
8. Try creating a new project based upon the **My Project Template**. Notice how none of the changes saved in **widgets** have affected the template.
9. Close the project file without saving but leave *Project* open for the next lesson.

Driving Lesson 30 - Revision

Park and Read

At the end of every section you get the chance to complete one or more revision exercises to develop your skills and prepare you for your ECDL certification test. You should aim to complete the following steps without referring back to the previous lessons.

Manoeuvres

1. Create a new project based on the **My Project Template** file. Set a **Start Date** for the project as *01/09/2017*.

2. Open the **Properties** dialog box and, on the **Summary** tab, change the subject text to **Moving office**.

3. Change the name of task **1**, **My Project Start**, to **Move office**.

4. Then change task **3**, **My Project Finish**, to **Move complete**.

5. Enter the following tasks between the milestones in row 1 and 3 (replacing **First Task Goes Here** in the process):

   Plan move
   Prepare new site
   Set up office
   Do the move

6. Insert two new rows <u>above</u> **Prepare new site** and add these new tasks:

   Research location
   Negotiate new lease

7. Delete task **2**, **Plan move**.

8. Check that your project plan matches the one shown below.

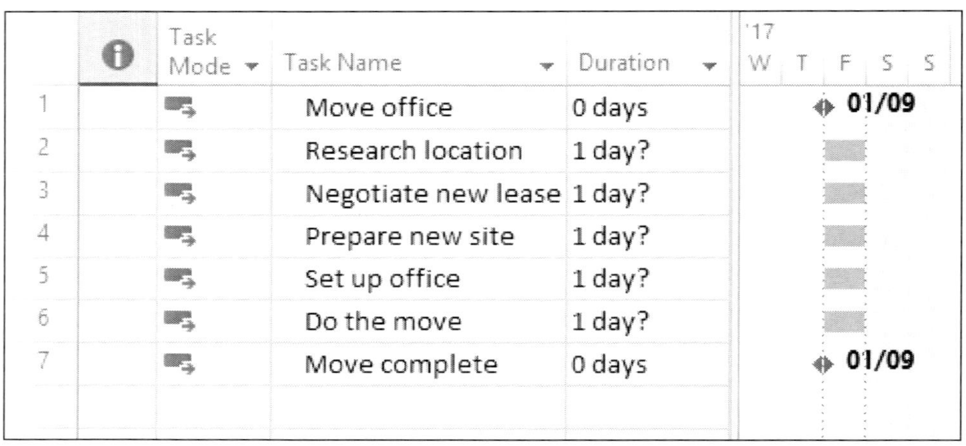

	Task Mode	Task Name	Duration
1		Move office	0 days
2		Research location	1 day?
3		Negotiate new lease	1 day?
4		Prepare new site	1 day?
5		Set up office	1 day?
6		Do the move	1 day?
7		Move complete	0 days

Driving Lesson 30 - Continued

9. Add the following durations:

Research location	**1 week**
Negotiate new lease	**1 week**
Prepare new site	**3 weeks**
Set up office	**6 days**
Do the move	**1 week**

10. Tasks **5** and **6** are in the wrong order. Swap them around.
11. Insert a new task above task **6**. Enter the name **Old site vacated**.
12. Make task **6**, **Old site vacated**, a milestone.

		Task Mode	Task Name	Duration
1			Move office	0 days
2			Research location	1 wk
3			Negotiate new lease	1 wk
4			Prepare new site	3 wks
5			Do the move	1 wk
6			Old site vacated	0 days
7			Set up office	6 days
8			Move complete	0 days

13. Save the project as **revision** in the data files folder (you will return to this later in the guide).
14. Save the project as a PDF file named **revision pdf** in the data files folder.

*A sample project can be found in the **Revisions** folder within the data files. You can use this to compare your work against a model solution.*

15. Open the project **section4 revision complete** within **Revisions** in the data files folder. Does the project plan match the one you created?
16. Close *Project* and any open files (without saving any changes).

*Now complete the **Record of Achievement Matrix** at the back of the guide. You should only move on when confident with the topics and features described in this section.*

Section 5 Subtasks

By the end of this section you should be able to:

Create, edit and delete subtasks

Work with subtasks

Understand summary tasks

Create recurring tasks

Work through the **Driving Lessons** in this section to gain an understanding of the above features.

For each **Driving Lesson**, read all of the **Park and Read** instructions and then, if applicable, perform the numbered steps of the **Manoeuvres**. Complete the **Revision** exercise(s) at the end of the section to test your knowledge.

Driving Lesson 31 - Creating Subtasks

Park and Read

Once you have defined the broad goals of a project, each high-level task should then be broken down into a list of more detailed **subtasks**. These subtasks describe how the high-level task will be achieved.

When you break a high-level task into subtasks, the original high-level task becomes known as a ***Summary Task****.*

Manoeuvres

1. Start *Project*.

On Project's *starting screen, you can click* ***Open Other Projects*** *on the left panel to display the* ***Open*** *screen.*

2. Open the project **movie** that you created earlier.

An up-to-date model copy of the ***movie*** *project is available in the data files folder* ***Training****. This is named* ***section5 movie****. If you would like to use this, open the project and save it as* ***movie*** *in the main data files folder.*

3. Insert 5 new rows above task **4**, **Raise finance**.

As with normal tasks, subtasks should be listed in the ***Task List*** *in the order that they will be performed.*

4. Add the following new tasks and their durations:

First draft	**3 days**
First review	**2 days**
Second draft	**3 days**
Second review	**2 days**
Complete script	**0 days**

5. Using the **Row Heading Bar**, select row **4**. Hold down <**Shift**> and click row **8**. Five rows are now selected at the same time.

Alternatively, you can click and drag across rows numbers on the ***Row Heading Bar*** *to select them.*

6. Click the **Indent Task** button, , in the **Schedule** group on the **TASK** tab to make the selected tasks subtasks of task **3**.

Driving Lesson 31 - Continued

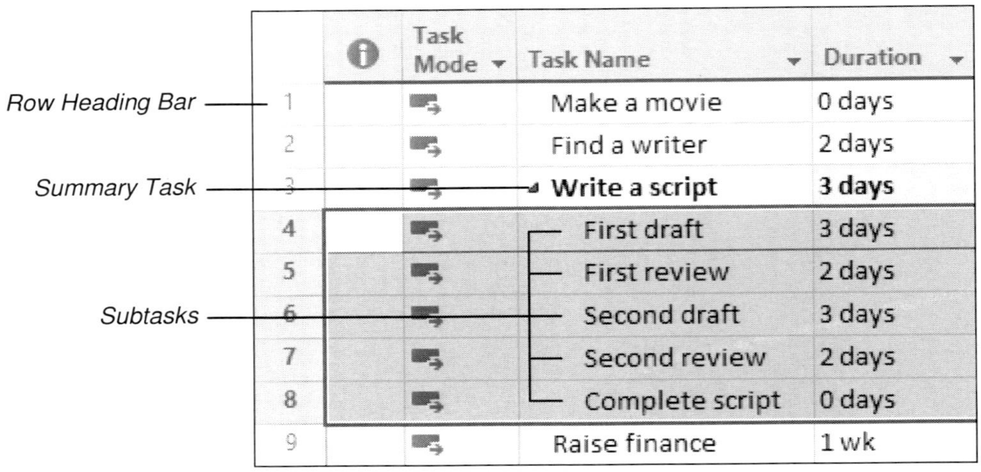

*Task **3** is now known as a **Summary Task** as it summarises the subtasks below it. Notice that the subtasks are indented slightly.*

*Notice also that task **3**, **Write a script** appears as a summary task bar on the **Gantt Chart**, ⌐¬. The duration of a summary task is the time taken to complete all of its subtasks (it does not have its own duration).*

7. Select task **9**, **Raise finance** and click the **Indent Task** button, . This "demotes" the task to become another subtask of task **3**.

8. With task **9** still selected, click the **Outdent Task** button, . This "promotes" the subtask to a normal task once again.

9. Select task **14**, **Review budget** and click the **Indent Task** button, . This "demotes" the task and turns task **13**, **Shoot movie** into a summary task instead.

10. With task **14** still selected, click the **Outdent Task** button, . Tasks **13** and **14** become normal tasks again.

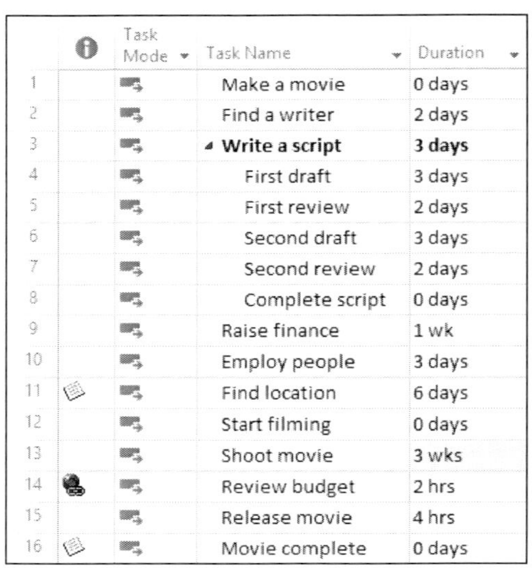

	Task Mode	Task Name	Duration
1		Make a movie	0 days
2		Find a writer	2 days
3		**Write a script**	**3 days**
4		First draft	3 days
5		First review	2 days
6		Second draft	3 days
7		Second review	2 days
8		Complete script	0 days
9		Raise finance	1 wk
10		Employ people	3 days
11		Find location	6 days
12		Start filming	0 days
13		Shoot movie	3 wks
14		Review budget	2 hrs
15		Release movie	4 hrs
16		Movie complete	0 days

Driving Lesson 32 - Displaying Subtasks

Park and Read

Different "levels" of subtasks can be hidden to show different amounts of detail in a project plan.

Manoeuvres

1. You can hide and show subtasks in the **Task List**. Click the **Expand/Collapse** button, ◢, to the left of task 3's task name.

2	Find a writer	2 days
3	◢ **Write a script**	**3 days**
4	First draft	3 days

2. The subtasks are hidden but the summary task remains.
3. Click the **Expand/Collapse** button again, ▷, to the left of task 3's task name to show the subtasks.
4. Save the project using the same file name, **movie**.
5. Close the project and then open the file **Subtasks**. This sample project shows a number of existing summary and subtasks.
6. Move your mouse pointer over the **Task Name** column header. The mouse pointer changes to ⬇.

		Task Name	Duration
1		Design a New Railway	25 days
2		◢ **Track Phase**	**27 days**

7. Click once on the **Task Name** field heading to select all task names.
8. Display the **VIEW** tab and click the **Outline** button in the **Data** group.
9. From the submenu that appears, select **Hide Subtasks**. Only the summary tasks are now shown.

		Task Name	Duration
1		Design a New Railway	25 days
2		▷ **Track Phase**	**27 days**
8		▷ **Station Phase**	**45 days**
16		Open New Line	0 days

Driving Lesson 32 - Continued

10. Select task **2**, **Track Phase** only. Drop down the **Outline** button again and, this time, click **Show Subtasks** to show the subtasks for this summary task only.

*Notice that you can have summary tasks within summary tasks. This allows you to create multiple **levels** of detail.*

11. Select task **5**, **Lay Track** and use the **Outline** button again to show subtasks for this summary task also.

*To display all subtasks in a project, click **Outline** and select **All Subtasks**.*

12. To view all project tasks, drop down the **Outline** button and select **All Subtasks**.

You can view all subtasks at a certain level of indentation. This can be used to increase or decrease the level of detail shown in a project plan.

13. Drop down the **Outline** button and select **Level 1**. Only level 1 tasks are now shown, displaying a very high-level view of the project.
14. Drop down the **Outline** button and select **Level 2**. Level 1 and level 2 tasks are now shown, displaying a more detailed view of the project.
15. Drop down the **Outline** button and select **Level 3**. Levels 1, 2 and 3 tasks are now shown displaying an even more detailed view of the project.

To quickly indent or "outdent" a task with the mouse, place the mouse pointer over the left side of the task name. The cursor changes to a double-headed arrow, ↔. Click and drag to the right to indent a task or to the left to outdent it.

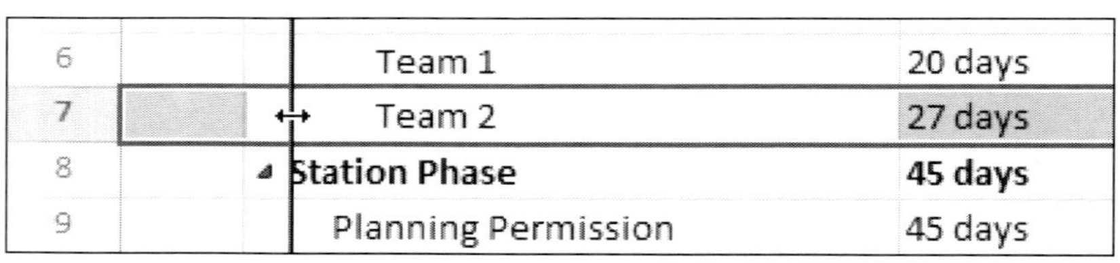

16. Experiment with indenting and outdenting tasks and changing the outline level.

*If a column's width is too narrow to display information (e.g. a **Task Name** is cut off), you can drag the boundary bars between column headers to resize them. Double-clicking a boundary bar will automatically adjust a column to the width of the widest item in that column. This technique also applies to row heights.*

17. When you are finished, close the project <u>without</u> saving.

Driving Lesson 33 - Recurring Tasks

Park and Read

In certain situations a task might recur throughout a project at regular set intervals (e.g. a monthly meeting). If this is the case, it can be set up as a **recurring** (repeating) task.

Manoeuvres

1. Open the project **movie** again.
2. Select task **2**, **Find a writer**. During the initial stages of the project, you want to conduct three weekly meetings with the production team. Let's create this as a recurring task.
3. On the **TASK** tab, click the drop-down arrow on the **Task** button in the **Insert** group. From the options that appear, select **Recurring Task**.

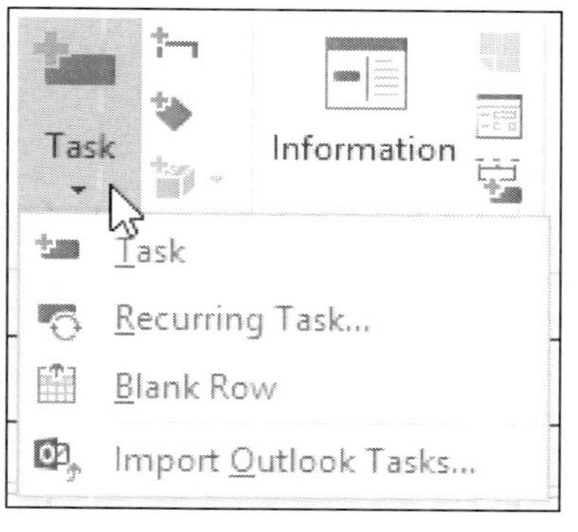

4. The **Recurring Task Information** dialog box appears. Enter the **Task Name** as **Production meetings** and enter a **Duration** of **2 hours**.
5. Select each of the options below **Recurrence pattern** and examine the settings that appear. These can be used to set how often a task repeats.
6. Choose to repeat the task **Weekly** on a **Monday**, as shown below.

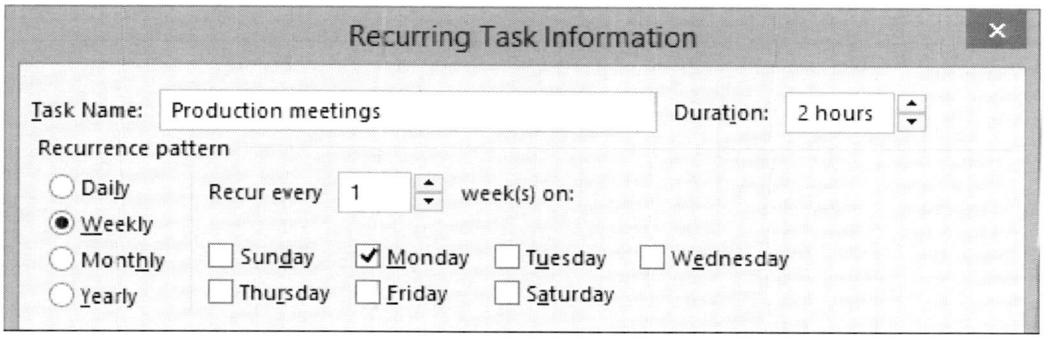

7. Notice the **Start**, **End after** and **End by** boxes. These can be used to set the range of the recurrence (i.e. how many times it will occur).

Driving Lesson 33 - Continued

8. Leave the **Start** date as it is (i.e. the start of the project) and select **End after**. Make sure **3 occurrences** is selected.

*If **End by** was selected,* Project *will create as many occurrences of this task as necessary to fill the time.*

9. Click **OK**. A summary task is created with 3 subtasks.

Recurrence icon

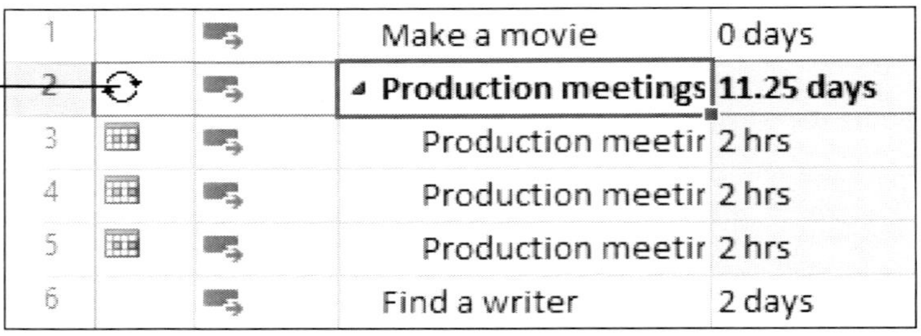

*Notice the recurrence icon for task **2** in the **Indicators** column.*

10. Rename the three recurring subtasks as follows:

    Meet Director
    Meet Producer
    Effects company

11. With task **2** selected, click the **Information** button to view the task's recurrence settings.

12. Change the recurrence to occur on **Wednesday** *instead* of Monday (remove Monday's selection) and click **OK**. The task is updated.

13. You've decided that it would be easier to meet with all of the production team at the same time. Select task **2**, **Production meetings** on the **Row Heading Bar** and press <**Delete**> to remove it.

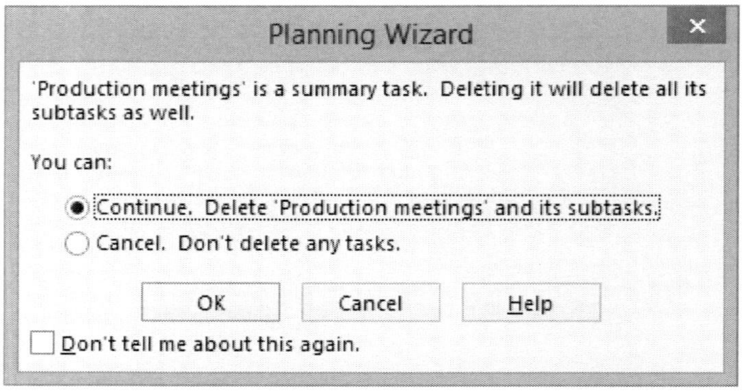

14. With **Continue. Delete 'Production meetings' and its subtasks** selected, click **OK**. The recurring tasks are all deleted.

15. Insert a new, normal task <u>above</u> task **2**, **Find a writer**. Name it **Production meeting** and give it a **Duration** of **2 hours**.

Driving Lesson 34 - Develop Your Skills

Park and Read

In this lesson you will add more detail to the **movie** project plan.

Manoeuvres

1. Insert three rows above task **11**, **Employ people** and add the following tasks and their durations:

Meet solicitors	**10 days**
Meet banks	**25 days**
Sign deal	**0 days**

2. Make the three new tasks subtasks of task **10**, **Raise finance**.
3. Next, insert three rows above task **16**, **Start filming** and add the following tasks and their durations:

Look locally	**10 days**
Look nationally	**15 days**
Confirm location	**0 days**

4. Make the three new tasks subtasks of task **15**, **Find location**.
5. Insert four rows above task **21**, **Review budget** and add the following tasks and their durations:

Erect set	**20 days**
Crew on set	**40 days**
Actors on set	**37 days**
Filming complete	**0 days**

6. Make the four new tasks subtasks of task **20**, **Shoot movie**.
7. Next, insert two rows above subtask **23**, **Actors on set** and add the following tasks and their durations

Hire technicians	**40 days**
Hire cameras	**40 days**

8. Make the two new tasks subtasks of task **22**, **Crew on set**.
9. On the **VIEW** tab, drop down the **Outline** button and select **Level 1**. Only level 1 tasks are shown (displaying a very high-level view of the project).
10. Use the **Outline** button and select **Level 2**. Both level 1 and level 2 tasks are shown. Finally, use the **Outline** button and select **All Subtasks**.
11. Save the **movie** project and close it.

Driving Lesson 35 - Revision

Park and Read

At the end of every section you get the chance to complete one or more revision exercises to develop your skills and prepare you for your ECDL certification test. You should aim to complete the following steps without referring back to the previous lessons.

Manoeuvres

1. Open the project **revision** that you created earlier.

*An up-to-date model copy of the **revision** project is available in the data files folder **Training**. This is named **section5 revision**. If you would like to use this, open the project and save it as **revision** in the main data files folder.*

2. Add three new tasks above task **3**, **Negotiate new lease**. Enter the following task names and durations:

Look locally	**2 days**
Look nationally	**3 days**
Confirm location	**0 days**

3. Make the three new tasks subtasks of task **2**, **Research location**.

4. Add three new tasks above task **7**, **Prepare new site**. Enter the following task names and durations:

Meet Estate Agents	**3 days**
Arrange finance	**2 day**
Sign deal	**0 days**

5. Make the three new tasks subtasks of task **6**, **Negotiate new lease**.

6. Add the two following new tasks above task **9**, **Sign deal**.

Meet banks	**1 day**
Meet investors	**1 day**

7. Make the two new tasks subtasks of task **8**, **Arrange finance**.

8. Adjust the width of the **Task Name** column in the **Task List** so that all task names can be fully seen.

Recall that, to resize a column, you can drag the boundary bars between column headers. Double-clicking a boundary bar will automatically adjust a column to the width of the widest item in that column.

Driving Lesson 35 - Continued

9. If necessary, adjust the width of the **Task Pane** so that the **Duration** column can be fully seen.

10. View only level 1 tasks. Then view only level 2 tasks. Finally, view all subtasks.

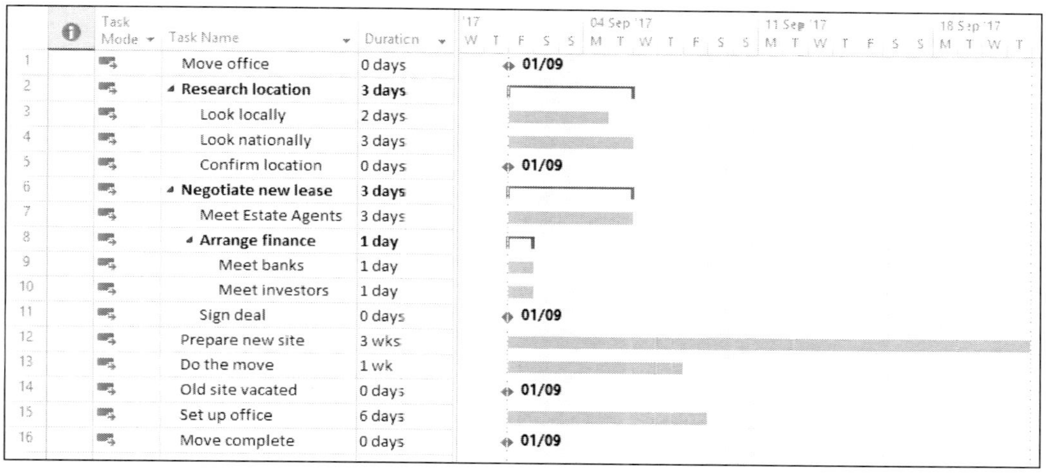

11. Save the project using the same filename (**revision**).

*A sample project named **section5 revision complete** can be found in the **Revisions** folder within the data files. You can use this to compare your work against a model solution.*

12. Close all open files but leave *Project* open for the next section.

*Now complete the **Record of Achievement Matrix** at the back of the guide. You should only move on when confident with the topics and features described in this section.*

Section 6
Linking Tasks

By the end of this section you should be able to:

Recognise link dependencies

Understand predecessors and successors

Link tasks

Unlink tasks

Link using task information

Adjust zoom levels

Work through the **Driving Lessons** in this section to gain an understanding of the above features.

For each **Driving Lesson**, read all of the **Park and Read** instructions and then, if applicable, perform the numbered steps of the **Manoeuvres**. Complete the **Revision** exercise(s) at the end of the section to test your knowledge.

Driving Lesson 36 - Task Dependencies

Park and Read

Once you have entered all of your project's tasks, you can then start **linking** them together to build a **schedule**. This creates **dependencies** between the start and end of tasks (i.e. the start or end of one task *depends* on the start or end of another).

In Project*, **dependencies** define the "relationships" between tasks.*

By default, linking tasks in *Project* creates **Finish-to-Start** (**FS**) task dependencies. As soon as the first task is finished, the following linked task(s) can start.

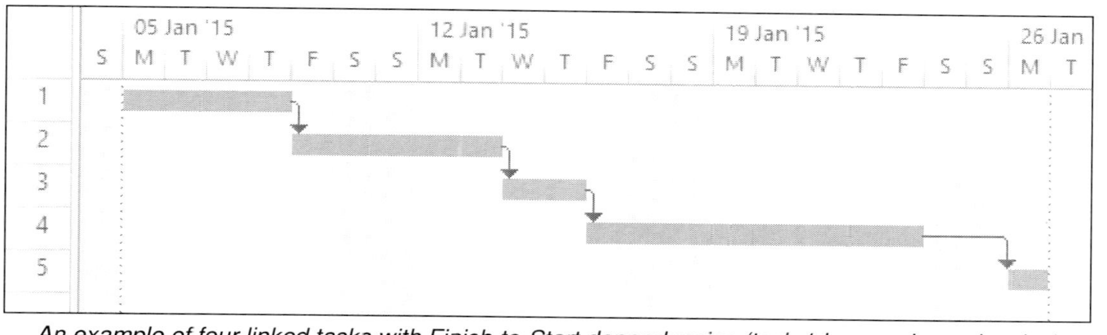

An example of four linked tasks with Finish-to-Start dependencies (task 1 has no dependencies)

*Dependencies are shown in the **Gantt Chart** as an arrow that links tasks, ↓. As the task dependencies are **Finish-to-Start**, the arrow shows the end of one task linking to the start of the next.*

You can also link tasks using **Start-to-Start** (**SS**) dependencies. As soon as the first task starts, the linked task(s) can also start.

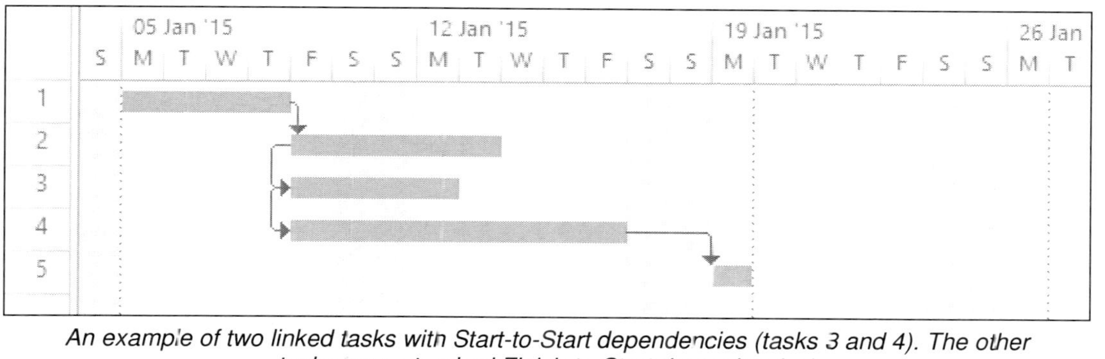

An example of two linked tasks with Start-to-Start dependencies (tasks 3 and 4). The other tasks have standard Finish-to-Start dependencies)

When tasks are auto-scheduled, Project *will use task durations and dependencies to automatically build your schedule. This is one of the most powerful and useful features of the application.*

***Finish-to-Start** and **Start-to-Start** are the two most popular types of dependency. Others include **Finish-to-Finish** (**FF**) and **Start-to-Finish** (**SF**).*

Driving Lesson 37 - Predecessors & Successors

Park and Read

As you have already learned, a task's start or end date can depend upon the start or end date of other related tasks. When tasks are linked to each other in this manner, they can be referred to as **predecessors** and **successors**.

The tasks upon which another task depends are known as **predecessors**. For example, actors needing to rehearse their lines in a movie require a script. *Writing a script* is therefore a predecessor (i.e. it comes before) *rehearse lines.*

*A **predecessor** is any task which has a start or finish date that determines the start or finish date of another task.*

Any delays or changes to a task will have an impact on all of the other tasks that depend on it. These dependent tasks are known as **successors**. For example, *rehearse lines* is a successor (i.e. it comes after) *writing a script.*

*A **successor** is a task which has a start or finish date determined by the start or finish date of another task.*

Examine the Gantt Chart below: the middle task is selected. The start of that task depends on the completion of the predecessor tasks above it. Similarly, the successor task afterwards depends on the selected task completing before it can start.

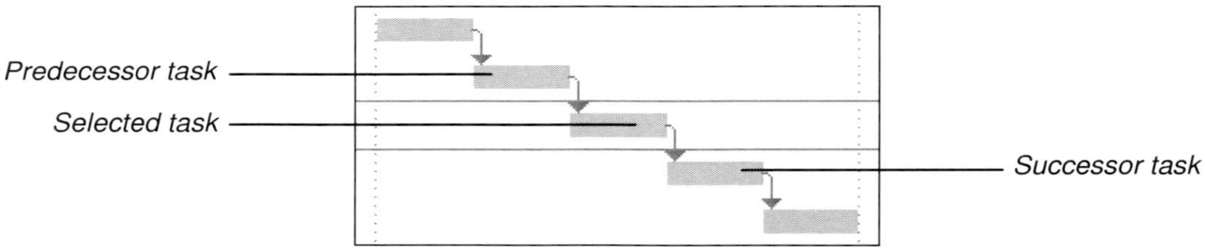

A task is always linked to a predecessor task to create a dependency (not the other way around).

Importantly, not all tasks in a project are necessarily related – many can occur simultaneously and are not necessarily affected by changes and delays to other tasks.

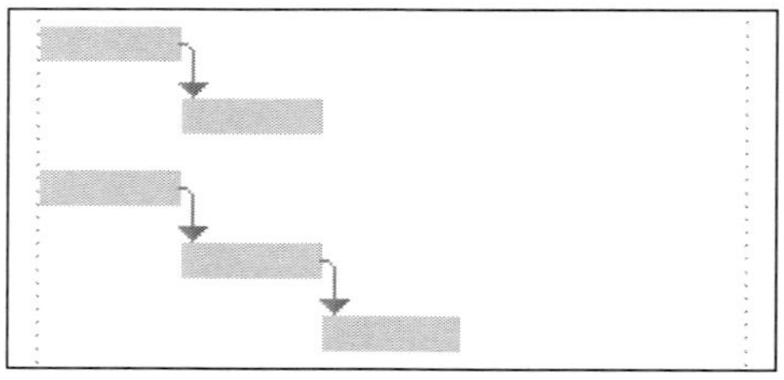

You will get to see these concepts in action in the lessons that follow...

Driving Lesson 38 - Finish-to-Start Links

Park and Read

The most common type of dependency between tasks is **Finish-to-Start**. A **Finish-to-Start** link is used when a task's start is dependent upon its predecessor finishing. The start of the task will be delayed if the predecessor's finish is delayed.

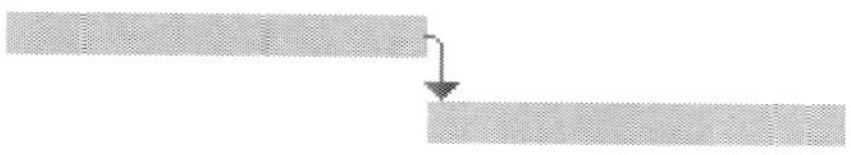

For example, a house building project requires the laying of foundations to be fully completed before any walls can be built on top. Therefore, laying foundations has to be *finished* before the bricklaying can start (the two tasks have a **Finish-To-Start** relationship).

Manoeuvres

1. Open the project **Links** from the data files folder. This project lists the four different types of dependency you can create in *Project*.

2. Select tasks **1** to **2** using the **Row Heading Bar**.

		Task Mode	Task Name	Duration
1			Finish-to-Start (Predecessor)	2 days
2			Finish-to-Start (Successor)	2 days
3				

3. Click the **Link the Selected Tasks** button, , in the **Schedule** group on the **TASK** tab.

4. The selected tasks are linked with a default **Finish-to-Start** dependency. Notice that the tasks are now linked in the **Gantt Chart**.

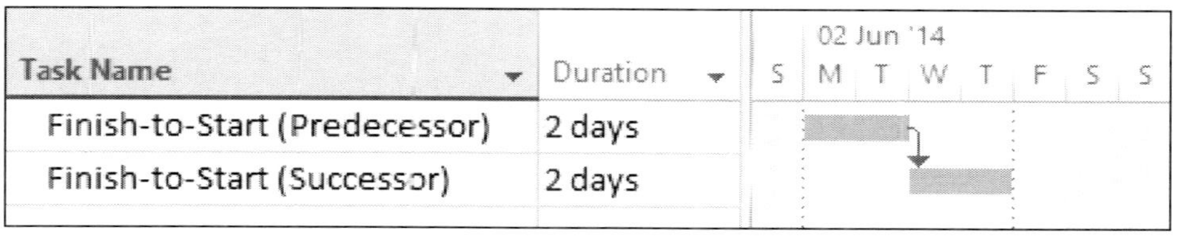

Task Name	Duration
Finish-to-Start (Predecessor)	2 days
Finish-to-Start (Successor)	2 days

5. Increase the duration of task **1** to **6 days**. Task **2**'s start date is delayed.

6. Now increase the duration of task **2** to **4** days. Notice that this has no effect on task **1**.

You can also select multiple rows at the same time to link. As you will see later, this is useful when you have a lot of tasks to link together at once.

Driving Lesson 39 - Start-to-Start Links

Park and Read

Another common type of dependency between tasks is **Start-to-Start**. This is used when a task has a start date dependent upon its predecessor's start date (i.e. it can't start until its predecessor starts). The task's start date will be delayed if its predecessor's start is delayed (but not vice versa).

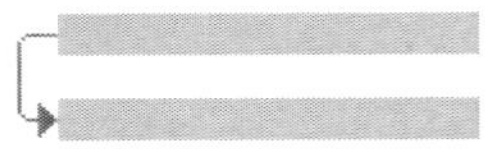

For example, the start of a train journey can only begin when a train driver's shift starts. The two tasks can therefore be linked with a **Start-to-Start** dependency. Delaying the start of the train driver's shift will delay the start of the train journey (but not vice versa).

Manoeuvres

1. The **Links** project should still be open. Select tasks **4** to **5** using the **Row Heading Bar**.

2. Click the **Link the Selected Tasks** button, , on the **TASK** tab. The selected tasks are linked with a **Finish-to-Start** dependency.

3. You now need to change task 5's dependency to **Start-to-Start**. Double click task **5** to show the **Task Information** box.

4. Select the **Predecessors** tab and notice that a **Finish-to-Start** link has been created to task **4**. Click on the **Type** box and then use the drop-down arrow to select **Start-to-Start (SS)**.

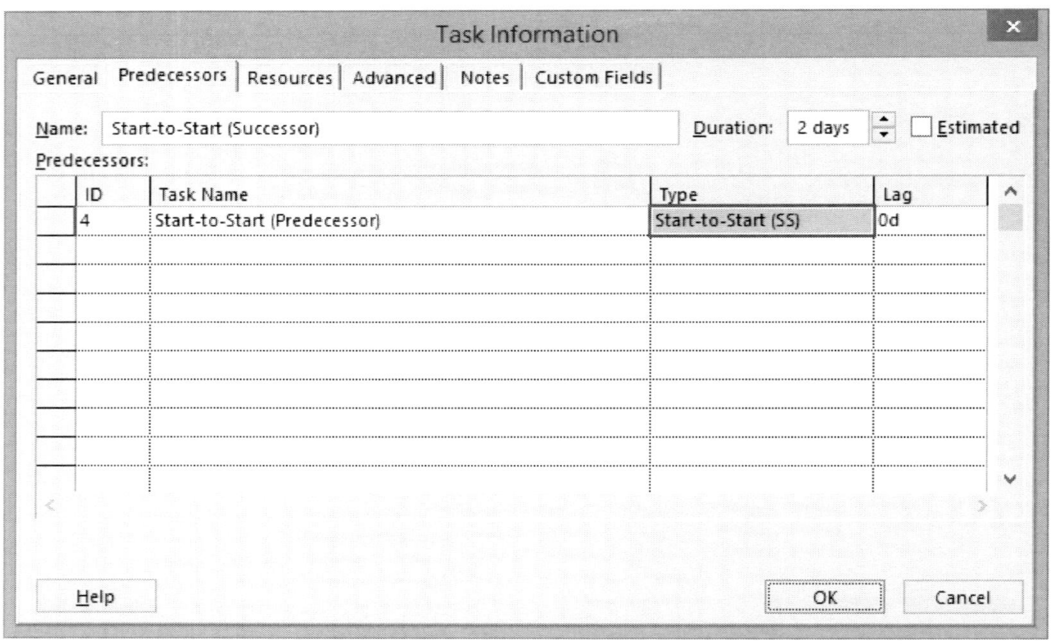

Driving Lesson 39 - Continued

*After clicking in the **Type** box, the required link can be quickly inserted by typing the initials of the link, i.e. **FS**, **SS**, **FF** or **SF**, followed by <**Enter**>.*

5. Click **OK**. Notice that the relationship between task **5** and its predecessor, task **4**, is now **Start-to-Start**.

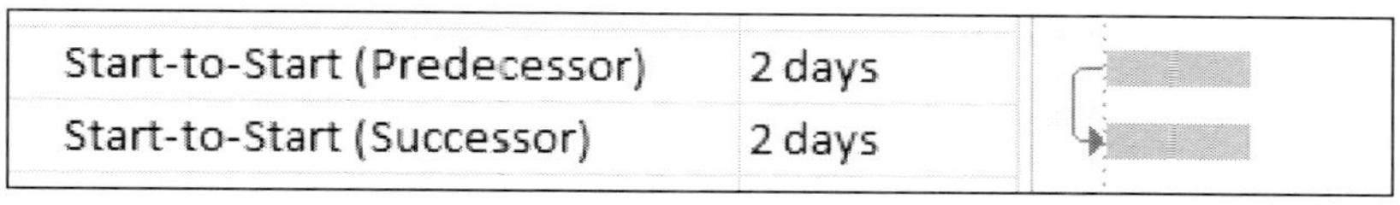

6. Change the duration of task **4** to **4 days**. Note that this does not affect the start of task **5**.
7. Change the duration of task **5** to **5 days**. Similarly, this does not affect the start of task **4**.

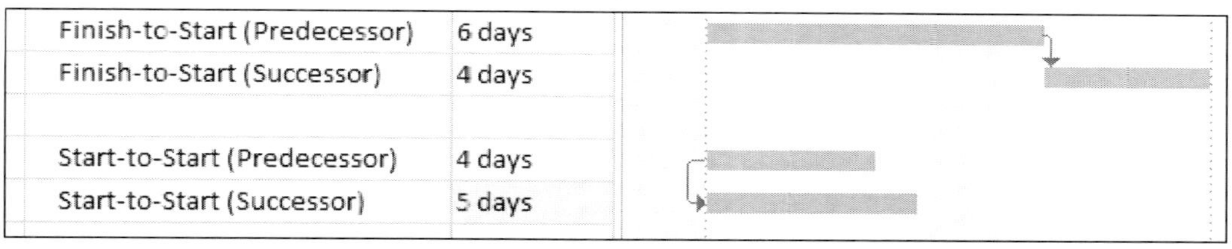

8. Leave the project open for the next lesson.

Driving Lesson 40 - Finish-to-Finish Links

Park and Read

A **Finish-to-Finish** link is used when a successor task has a finish date dependent upon the finish of its predecessor. Any delay in the finishing of the predecessor will delay the finishing of the successor.

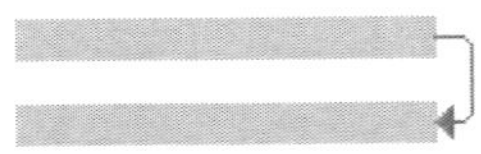

For example, in a building project, the task of providing a security patrol must continue until the task of building a perimeter wall is complete. The security patrol task can, therefore, be linked to the perimeter wall building task with a **Finish-to-Finish** relationship. If finishing the wall is delayed, then the security patrol task must be extended.

Manoeuvres

1. The **Links** project should still be open. Select tasks **7** to **8** using the **Row Heading Bar**.
2. Click the **Link the Selected Tasks** button, . The selected tasks are once again linked with a default **Finish-to-Start** dependency.
3. You now need to change task 8's dependency to **Finish-to-Finish**. Select task **8** only and then open the **Task Information** dialog box.
4. Select the **Predecessors** tab and notice that a **Finish-to-Start** link has been created to task **7**. Click on the **Type** box and then use the drop-down arrow to select **Finish-to-Finish (FF)**.
5. Click **OK**. Notice that the relationship between task **8** and its predecessor, task **7**, is now **Finish-to-Finish**.
6. Change the duration of task **7** to **5 days**. Note the effect it has on the start of task **8**.
7. Change the duration of task **8** to **4 days**. Note that this does not affect the start of task **7** but has altered the start of task **8**.

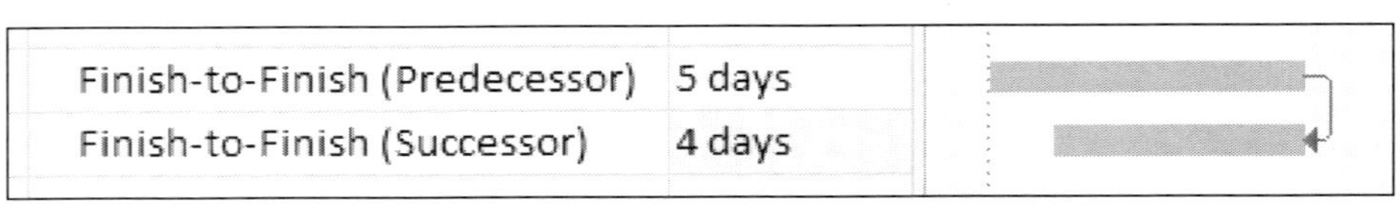

8. Leave the project open for the next lesson.

Driving Lesson 41 - Start-to-Finish Links

Park and Read

A **Start-to-Finish** link is used when a successor task has a finish date dependent upon the start of its predecessor. Any delay in the start of the predecessor will delay the finish of its successor.

For example, the provision of ground support to the crew in a space shuttle launch must continue until the second that the launch process starts. Therefore the ground support is linked to the launch process with a **Start-to-Finish** link. If the start of the launch is delayed, then the ground support task must be extended.

Manoeuvres

1. The **Links** project should still be open. Select tasks **10** to **11** using the **Row Heading Bar**.
2. Click the **Link the Selected Tasks** button, .
3. You now need to change task 11's dependency to **Start-to-Finish**. Select task **11** only and then display the **Task Information** dialog box.
4. Select the **Predecessors** tab and notice that a **Finish-to-Start** link has been created to task **10**. Click on the **Type** box and then use the drop-down arrow to select **Start-to-Finish (SF)**.
5. Click **OK**. Because of the dependency type, task **11** will now begin before task **10** (and therefore before the start of the project). This would normally be silly – tasks shouldn't start before the project begins – but for demonstration purposes click **OK**.
6. Notice that the relationship between task **11** and its predecessor, task **10**, is now **Start-to-Finish**. Change the duration of task **10** to **5 days**. Note that this does not affect the start of either task.
7. Change the duration of task **11** to **4 days**. Note the effect on the start of task **11** – it now starts earlier.
8. Save the project as **links complete** and close it.

*Although it is useful to know about **Finish-to-Finish** and **Start-to-Finish** dependency types, you will rarely use these in practise. For the ECDL certification test, you will only need to create simple **Finish-to-Start** and **Start-to-Start** links.*

Driving Lesson 42 - Gantt Chart Links

Park and Read

You can also create links between tasks using the **Gantt Chart**. To do this, simply drag one task bar onto another.

Manoeuvres

1. Start a new, blank project. The start date, by default, is set to today. This is okay for the purposes of this lesson.

2. Use the **Status Bar** to change the creation of new tasks to **AUTO SCHEDULED**.

3. Enter the following tasks and their durations:

Book holiday	**4 days**
Fly out	**2 days**
Get to hotel	**1 day**
Sit in sun	**7 days**
Spend money	**5 days**
Get to airport	**1 day**
Fly home	**2 day**

*By default, a project's end date is the date that the final task is completed. As all tasks in the current project plan currently start today, the project's end date will occur when the longest task, tasks **4**, completes.*

4. Move your mouse pointer over the centre of task **1**'s bar on the **Gantt Chart**. The pointer changes to a four-headed arrow.

5. Click and drag the very centre of the bar downwards towards task **2**'s bar. The mouse pointer changes to a link pointer, and a **ToolTip** appears showing the type of link that you are creating.

Finish-to-Start Link	
From Finish Of:	Task 1
To Start Of:	Task 2

6. When the link pointer is over the very centre of task **1**'s bar on the **Gantt Chart** (as shown below), release the mouse button.

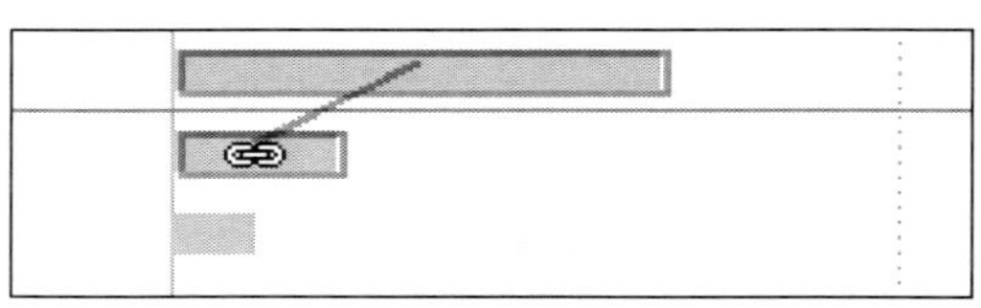

7. Task **2** is now linked to task **1** with a default **Finish-to-Start** dependency.

Driving Lesson 42 - Continued

*If you make a mistake, simply use the **Undo** button, , and try again.*

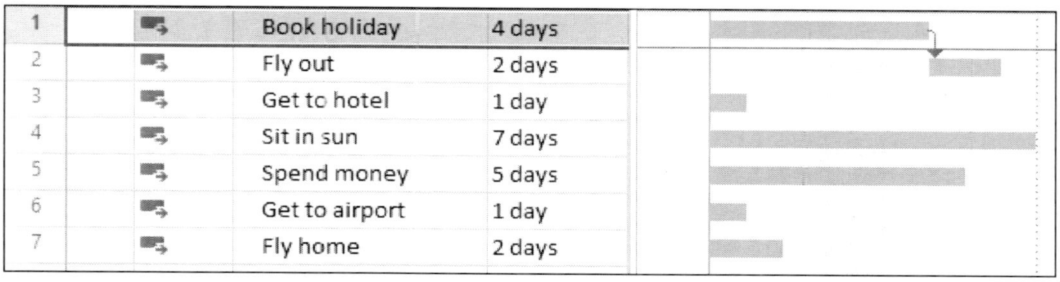

8. Use the same technique to link task **2** to task **3**.

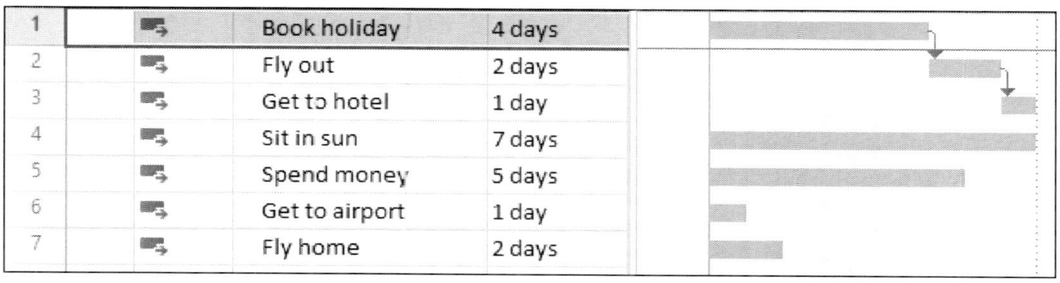

9. Save the project as **holiday**.
10. Leave the project open for the next lesson.

Driving Lesson 43 - Task Information Links

Park and Read

Tasks can also be linked using the **Task Information** dialog box.

Manoeuvres

1. The **holiday** project should be still open from the previous lesson.

2. Select task **4**, **Sit in sun**. Then open the **Task Information** dialog box and display the **Predecessors** tab.

*Notice that the **Predecessors** table is empty – this task is currently not linked to any predecessor task.*

3. Click on the first empty **ID** box and type **3** (i.e. task **3**). Press <**Enter**> to complete the link and the additional task information boxes will be automatically completed.

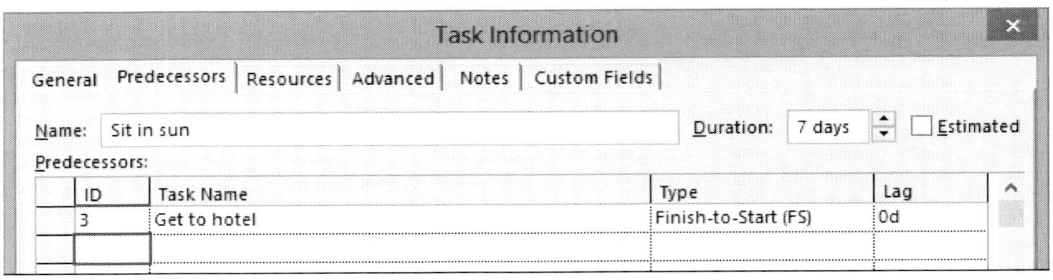

*The **Task Information** dialog box is used to link a task to one or more predecessors (not the other way around).*

4. Click **OK** to create a default **Finish-to-Start** link.

5. Double click on task **5** in the **Task List** to display the **Task Information** dialog box.

6. On the **Predecessors** tab, link this task to task **4**. This time, select a **Start-to-Start** link under **Type**. Click **OK**.

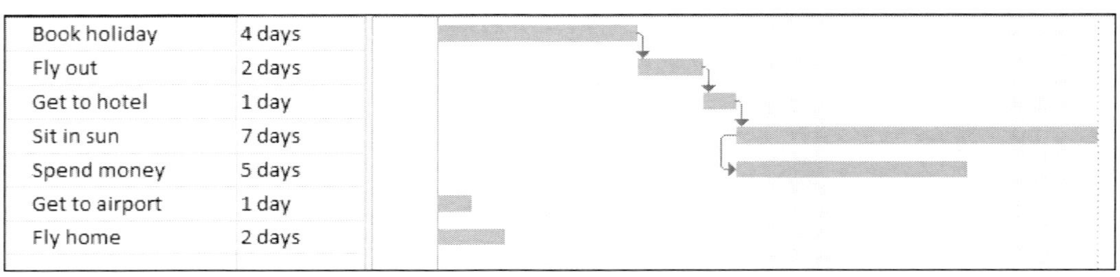

*Tasks do not need to be linked in the order that they appear in the **Task List**. That is, you can link any task to any other task in any order that makes sense.*

Driving Lesson 43 - Continued

7. Next, use the **Task Information** dialog box to create a **Finish-to-Start** link between task **6** and task **4**.

*Notice that the start date of task **6** is now dependent on the finish date of task **4**. It is not dependent on task **5** in any way.*

8. Finally, create another **Finish-to-Start** link between task **7** and task **6**.

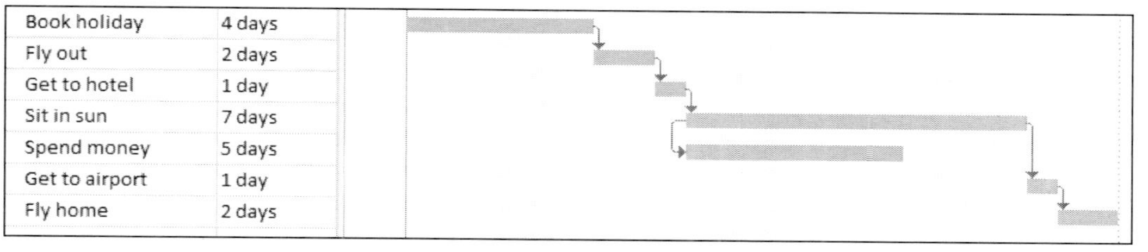

9. Good work. Save the project and close it.

Driving Lesson 44 - Changing Links

Park and Read

During a project, you may find that dependencies between tasks change and develop. If this happens, the links in your plan can be changed or deleted.

Manoeuvres

1. Open the project **Car**. This small project was created to help find, choose and then buy a new car.
2. Examine the links in the **Task List** and notice the different types of links between them. There are a number of errors that need to be corrected – can you tell what they are?
3. Firstly, task **6** is linked to task **5** with a **Start-to-Start** dependency. This doesn't make much sense (task **5** needs to be completed before task **6** starts). Double-click the link between task **5** and **6** on the **Gantt Chart** to open the **Task Dependency** dialog box.

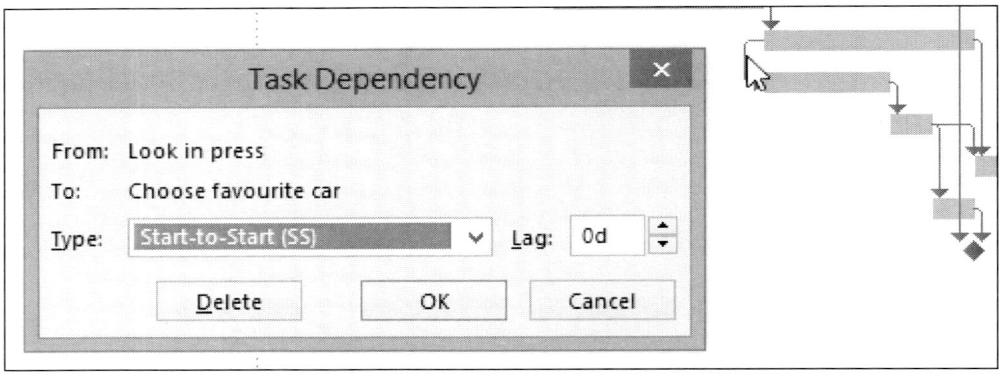

*If the **Bar Styles** dialog box appears, you did not click the link between tasks correctly. Click **Cancel** and then try again.*

4. On the **Task Dependency** dialog box, change the **Type** to **Finish-to-Start (FS)** and click **OK**. This corrects the error.

*A more comprehensive method of editing links is to display the **Task Information** dialog box. The type of link can be changed and new links created to additional tasks.*

5. Task **9** is linked to task **7**, but it should be linked to task **8**. Select task **9** in the **Task List** and display the **Task Information** dialog box.
6. On the **Predecessors** tab, click once on task **7** in the **ID** column. Then type **8** instead to overtype this and press <**Enter**>.
7. Click **OK** and the error is corrected.

Driving Lesson 44 - Continued

8. Next, notice that tasks **3**, **4** and **5** are all linked with **Finish-to-Start** dependencies. However, all three can occur at the same time. Let's change these links.

9. Select task **4** in the **Task List** and open the **Task Information** dialog box. On the **Predecessors** tab, notice that this task is currently linked to task **3** with a **Finish-to-Start** dependency.

10. Click once on **Finish-to-Start (FS)** in the **Type** column. Using the **Type** drop-down button that appears, ▾, select **Start-to-Start (SS)**.

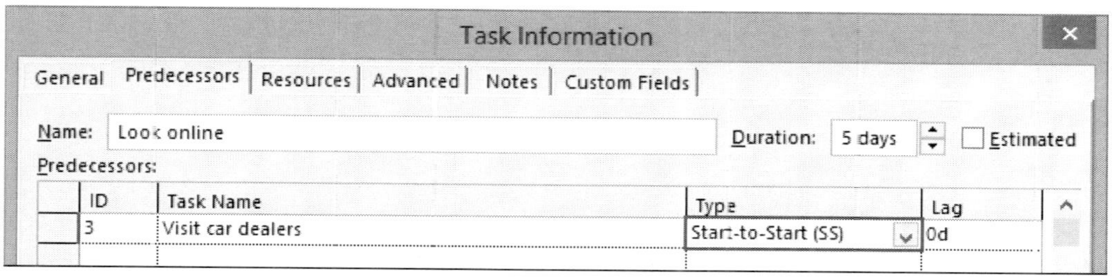

11. Click **OK**. Task **4** now starts at the same time as task **3**.

12. Use either the **Task Information** or **Task Dependency** dialog boxes to change the dependency between task **5** and **4** to **Start-to-Start** also.

13. Task **8** is incorrectly linked to task **5**. Double-click the link between task **8** and **5** on the **Gantt Chart** to open the **Task Dependency** dialog box.

14. Click the **Delete** button, Delete, to remove this link.

*You can also remove a link to a predecessor by selecting it on the **Task Information** dialog box's **Predecessors** tab and pressing <**Delete**>.*

15. Finally, the milestone at task **10** is incorrectly linked to task **3**. Select task **10** in the **Task List** and open the **Task Information** dialog box. On the **Predecessors** tab, click once on **Look Online** in the **Task Name** column.

16. Press <**Delete**> to remove the link. Then click **OK**.

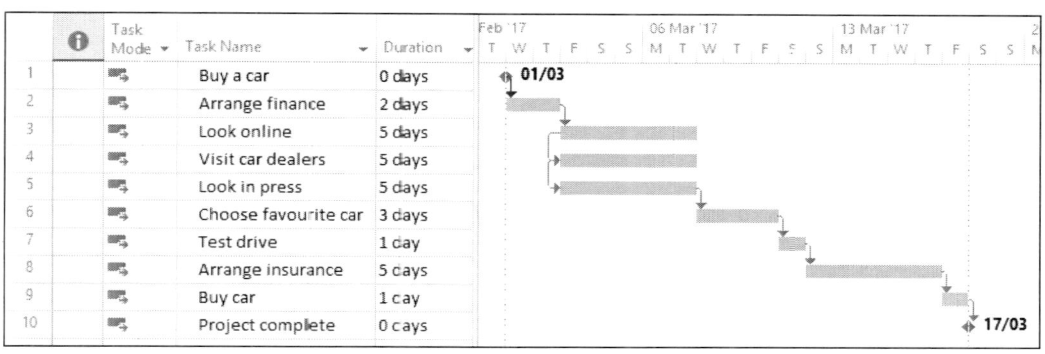

17. The project looks great. Save it as **car complete** and leave it open for the next lesson.

Driving Lesson 45 - Maintaining Links

Park and Read

Once you have created a chain of linked tasks, you will often find that you need to insert or delete a task that is dependent on those around it. By default, these new tasks will need to be manually "re-linked".

Manoeuvres

1. Using **car complete**, insert a new task <u>above</u> task **5**, **Look in press**.

2. Name the new task **Visit an auction** and give it a **Duration** of **1** day. Notice that the new task is not linked to any other task.

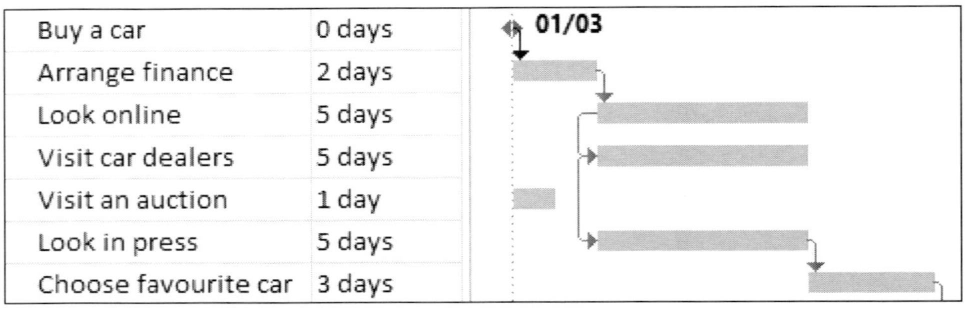

3. Select task **5** in the **Task List**. Then, open the **Task Information** dialog box and display the **Predecessors** tab.

4. Enter **4** in the **ID** column's first row and press <**Enter**>. A **Finish-to-Start** link to task **4**, **Visit car dealers** is created. Change the dependency **Type** to **Start-to-Start** so that it starts at the same time.

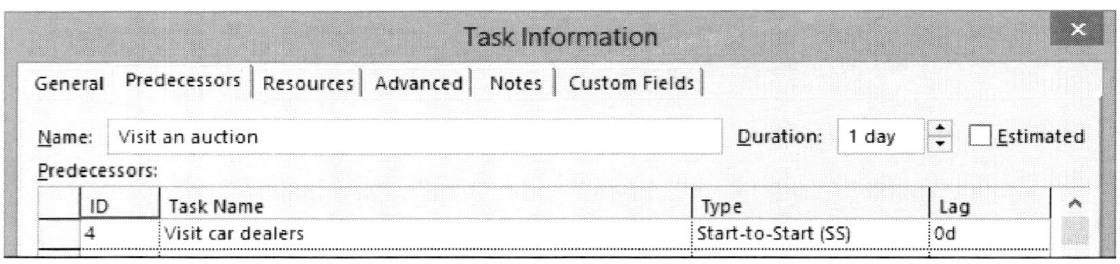

5. Click **OK** and the task is linked.

6. Notice that task **6** is still linked to task **4**. Change this so that task **6** has a **Start-to-Start** dependency with task **5** instead.

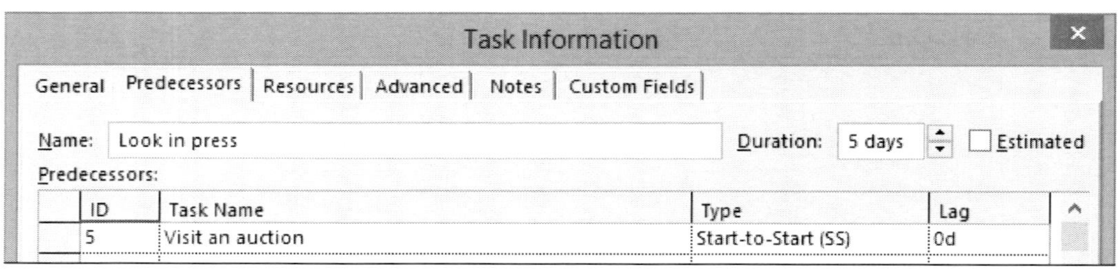

Driving Lesson 45 - Continued

7. Next, insert a new task <u>above</u> task **10**, **Buy car**. Name the new task **Pay road tax** and give it a **Duration** of **1 day**.

8. Link this task with a **Finish-to-Start** dependency with task **9**, **Arrange insurance**.

9. Then change task **11**, **Buy car**, so that it links to task **10** instead of **9**.

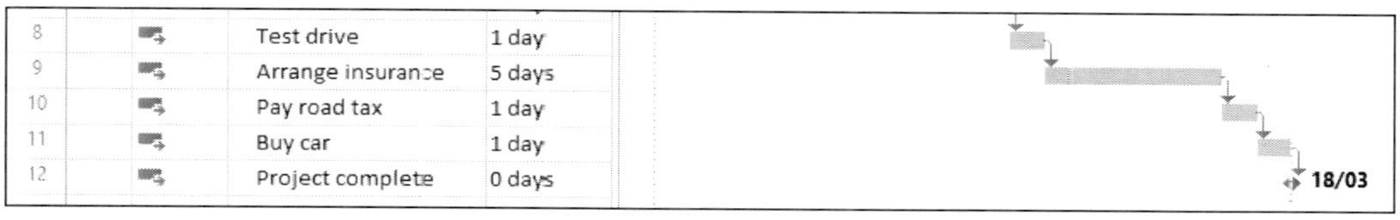

*The **Unlink Tasks** button, , in the **Schedule** group can be used to completely remove all predecessor and successor task links.*

10. Select task **8**, **Test drive**. Then click the **Unlink Tasks** button, , in the **Schedule** group on the **TASK** tab. All links to predecessor and successor tasks are removed.

11. Replace the **Finish-to-Start** dependency between task **9** and task **8**. Then link task **8** with task **7** again (**Finish-to-Start**).

*Recall that you can quickly create links between tasks using the **Gantt Chart**. To do this, simply drag one task bar onto another.*

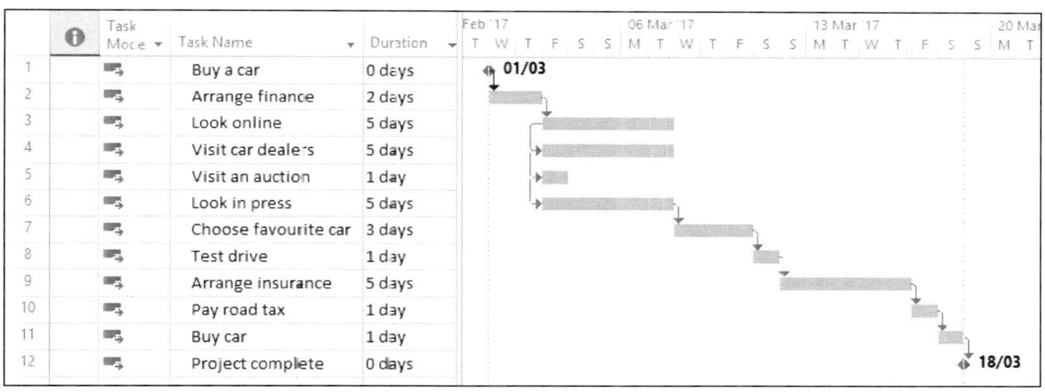

12. The project should now appear as shown above. Save it and leave it open for the next lesson.

Driving Lesson 46 - Best Practice

Park and Read

All project plans must accurately model real-life activities and events if they are to be of any use. It is therefore very important that you link tasks correctly with the most suitable dependency types.

Manoeuvres

1. Examine the **car complete** project. Tasks **4**, **5** and **6** are currently linked to their predecessors using **Start-to-Start** dependencies.

2. However, consider what would happen if your computer broke down and the start of task **3**, **Look online**, was delayed. All successor tasks would also be delayed, which doesn't make much sense.

3. It would be more logical for tasks **4**, **5** and **6** to be linked to task **2** with standard **Finish-to-Start** dependencies instead. Change tasks **4**, **5** and **6** – one at a time – to do this.

Predecessors:

ID	Task Name	Type
2	Arrange finance	Finish-to-Start (FS)

4. Examine the **Gantt Chart** and notice that tasks **4**, **5** and **6** are now linked to their predecessors using **Finish-to-Start** dependencies. This makes a lot more sense.

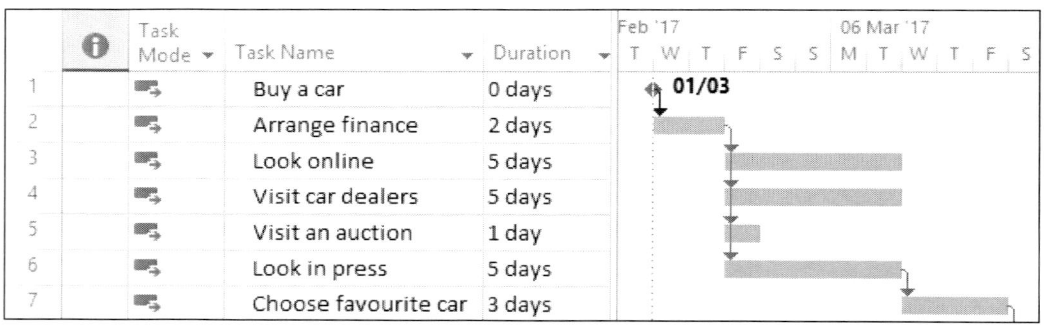

5. Increase the **Duration** of task **5** to **7 days** and notice the effect. Task **7** starts before task **5** has completed, which is clearly not right. In fact, task **7** should not start until tasks **3** to **6** have all completed.

6. Select task **7** and open the **Task Information** dialog box. On the **Predecessors** tab, notice that this task is currently linked to task **6**.

7. On the row below, enter **3** in the **ID** column and press <**Enter**> to create a default **Finish-to-Start** dependency. In the two rows below, create similar links to tasks **4** and **5** (as shown on the following page).

Driving Lesson 46 - Continued

8. Click **OK** and notice the effect. Task **7** now starts after tasks **3**, **4**, **5** and **6** have <u>all</u> completed.

9. Increase the **Duration** of task **3** to **10 days**. Task **7** starts even later.

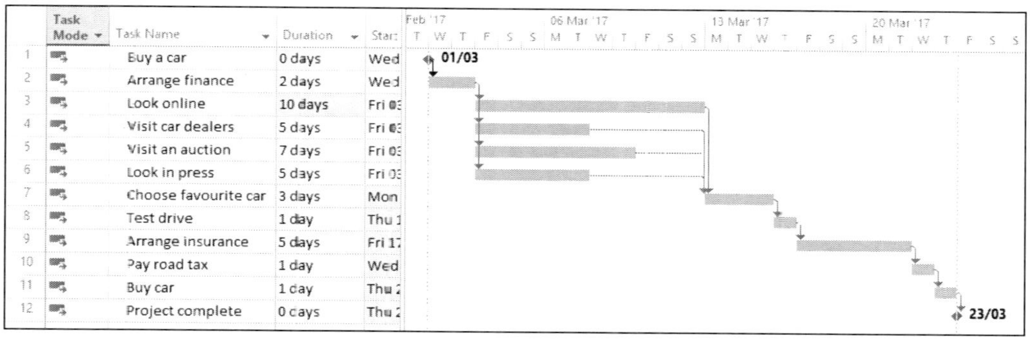

10. Save the project and close it.

Driving Lesson 47 - Adjusting Zoom Levels

Park and Read

As you add more and more tasks to your project, the **Gantt Chart** can become increasingly complex and difficult to view. To allow you to see more or less detail, you can adjust the **zoom** level.

Manoeuvres

1. Open the file **Railway**. This complex project plan shows the tasks needed to design and build a new railway. These tasks have been broken down into a number of summary tasks and subtasks.

2. Notice that the **Gantt Chart** is currently far too wide to fit on your screen. Use the horizontal scrollbar to scroll to the right and see more of it.

*You can adjust the zoom of the **Gantt Chart** to display all of the project at once.*

3. Display the **VIEW** tab and click the **Zoom Entire Project** button, , in the **Zoom** group. The **Gantt Chart** zooms out so that the entire project can be seen.

4. You can also manually zoom in and out of the **Gantt Chart**. Click the **Zoom** button, , in the **Zoom** group and select **Zoom In**. You can now see a greater amount of detail.

*Notice that the time interval markers on the **Timescale** bar at the top of the **Gantt Chart** change depending on the zoom level selected. The higher the zoom, the smaller the time intervals.*

5. Continue to use **Zoom In** until no further changes take place. The timescale bar will show the hours of a day split into 15-minute intervals.

6. Click the **Zoom** button and then **Zoom Out** to see more of the overall the project.

7. Continue to use **Zoom Out** until no further changes take place. The timescale bar will show numerous years split into halves.

8. Locate the **Zoom Slider** on the **Status Bar**, . Then try dragging the slider to the left (to zoom out) and right (to zoom in).

9. Use the **Zoom Entire Project** button, , to see all of the project.

10. Click the **Zoom** button, , in the **Zoom** group and select **Zoom**. You can use the **Zoom** dialog box to select a specific zoom level. As an example, select **1 week** and click **OK**. Notice the effect.

11. Close the project <u>without</u> saving.

Driving Lesson 48 - Develop Your Skills

Park and Read

In this lesson you will add more detail to the **movie** project plan. Take care and make sure you follow each step as accurately as you can.

Manoeuvres

1. Open the project **movie** that you created earlier.

*An up-to-date model copy of the **movie** project is available in the data files folder **Training**. This is named **section6 movie**. If you would like to use this, open the project and save it as **movie** in the main data files folder.*

2. Select tasks **1**, **2** and **3** together. Recall that you can select multiple rows using the **Row Heading Bar**.
3. Then, use the **Link the Selected Tasks** button, [button], to create **Finish-to-Start** links between them.
4. Next, select the following groups of tasks – one group at a time – and link them together using the **Link the Selected Tasks** button:

   Task 5 through to 9 (i.e. tasks **5**, **6**, **7**, **8** and **9**)

   Task 11 through to 13

   Task 16 through to 18

5. Using **Finish-to-Start** dependencies, link the following tasks (two tasks at a time):

   Tasks 3 and 5

   Tasks 9 and 11

   Tasks 13 and 14

   Tasks 14 and 16

   Tasks 18 and 19

You may find it easier to link a lot of tasks at once and then refine their links and dependency types afterwards.

6. Select the group of tasks **21** through to **29** together. Then, use the **Link the Selected Tasks** button to link them.
7. Link tasks **19** and **21** with a **Finish-to-Start** dependency.
8. It is now difficult to see all of the **Gantt Chart**. Display the **VIEW** tab and click the **Zoom Entire Project** button in the **Zoom** group.
9. Change the link between tasks **11** and **12** to **Start-to-Start**.

Driving Lesson 48 - Continued

10. Change the link between tasks **23** and **24** to **Start-to-Start**.

It is considered bad practice to link summary tasks together – in complex projects, the final subtask may look abandoned as it will not appear to link to anything.

11. Select task **22** and click the **Unlink Tasks** button, , in the **Schedule** group on the **TASK** tab.
12. Then, link tasks **21** and **23** with a **Finish-to-Start** dependency.
13. Link tasks **24** and **25** with a **<u>Start-to-Start</u>** dependency.
14. Finally, link tasks **26** and **27** with a **Finish-to-Start** dependency.
15. Task **26** is currently only linked to task **25**. Link task **26** to tasks **23** and **24** also with **Finish-to-Start** dependencies.
16. Display the **VIEW** tab and click the **Zoom Entire Project** button in the **Zoom** group.
17. All tasks are now correctly linked. Notice that the movie's end date is **09/06/2017**, as shown by the final milestone.

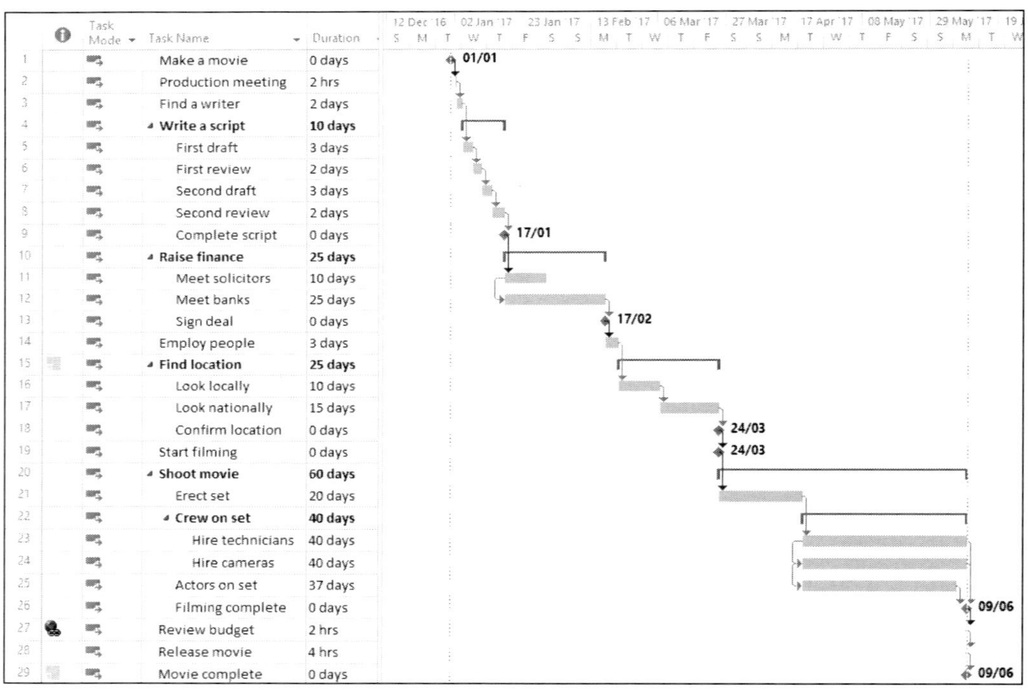

18. Save the project and close it.

Driving Lesson 49 - Revision

Park and Read

At the end of every section you get the chance to complete one or more revision exercises to develop your skills and prepare you for your ECDL certification test. You should aim to complete the following steps without referring back to the previous lessons.

Manoeuvres

1. Open the project **revision** that you created earlier.

*An up-to-date model copy of the **revision** project is available in the data files folder **Training**. This is named **section6 revision**. If you would like to use this, open the project and save it as **revision** in the main data files folder.*

2. Insert the following three tasks <u>above</u> task **13**, **Do the move**:

Builders	**2 weeks**
Decorators	**1 week**
Fitters	**1 week**

3. Make the new tasks subtasks of task **12**, **Prepare new site**.
4. Add the following five tasks <u>above</u> task **17**, **Old site vacated**:

Distribute boxes	**1 day**
Pack computers	**2 days**
Pack equipment	**3 days**
Hire removal co.	**1 day**
Transport boxes	**1 day**

5. Make the new tasks subtasks of task **16**, **Do the move**.
6. Next, select the following groups of tasks – one group at a time – and link them together with **Finish-to-Start** dependencies:

   Task 3 through to 5 (i.e. tasks **3**, **4** and **5**)
   Task 7 through to 11
   Task 13 through to 15
   Task 17 through to 24

7. Using **Finish-to-Start** dependencies, link the following tasks:

   Tasks 1 and 3
   Tasks 5 and 7
   Tasks 11 and 13
   Tasks 15 and 17

Driving Lesson 49 - Continued

8. Display the **VIEW** tab and click the **Zoom Entire Project** button in the **Zoom** group.
9. Task **10** should start at the same time as task **9**. Change the link to a **Start-to-Start** dependency.
10. Change the link between task **14** and **15** to **Start-to-Start**.
11. Task **11** is currently linked to a summary task, which is not recommended. Change the predecessor link for task **11** from **8** to **10** (**Finish-to-Start**).
12. Create a **Finish-to-Start** link between tasks **7** and **9**. Then, remove the predecessor for task **8** which links to a summary task.
13. Insert the following four tasks above task **24**, **Move complete**:

Unpack boxes	**1 day**
Arrange office	**3 days**
Assemble computers	**1 day**
Set up equipment	**2 days**

14. Select the four new tasks, create default **Finish-to-Start** links between them, and make them subtasks of task **23**, **Set up office**.
15. Correct any linking issues caused by adding tasks **24** to **27** (hint: summary tasks should not be linked, only subtasks).
16. Check the date of the final milestone, **Move complete**. It should occur on **25/10/2017**.
17. Save the project.

*A sample project named **section6 revision complete** can be found in the **Revisions** folder within the data files. You can use this to compare your work against a model solution.*

18. Close all open files but leave *Project* open for the next section.

*Now complete the **Record of Achievement Matrix** at the back of the guide. You should only move on when confident with the topics and features described in this section.*

Section 7
Lag, Lead & Elapsed Time

By the end of this section you should be able to:

Understand lag and lead

Add and edit lag time

Add and edit lead time

Use elapsed time

Work through the **Driving Lessons** in this section to gain an understanding of the above features.

For each **Driving Lesson**, read all of the **Park and Read** instructions and then, if applicable, perform the numbered steps of the **Manoeuvres**. Complete the **Revision** exercise(s) at the end of the section to test your knowledge.

Driving Lesson 50 - Lag Time

Park and Read

Lag time can be used to delay the start of a task. By adding lag time, there will be a delay between a predecessor task finishing and its successor starting.

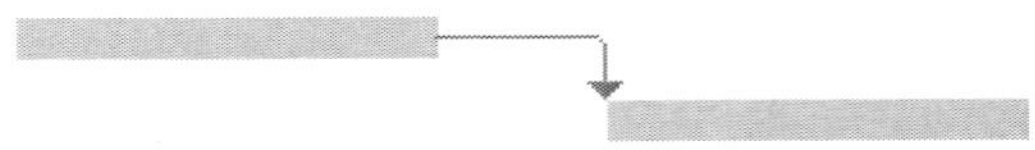

For example, on a house building project, you may want to leave two days between the pouring of concrete foundations and the building of a wall (to allow time for the concrete to dry). To do this, you can add lag time to the *wall building* task to delay its start.

Manoeuvres

1. Open the project **Lag and Lead**. Notice that there are eight pairs of linked tasks; two pairs for each of the four types of task dependency. Let's add a two-day lag time between the first pairing of each type.

2. Double-click the link between tasks **1** and **2** on the **Gantt Chart**. The **Task Dependency** dialog box appears.

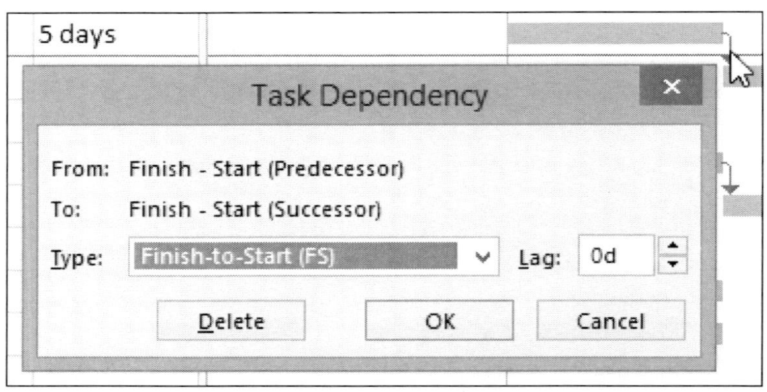

3. Notice that these two tasks are linked with a **Finish-to-Start** dependency. Use the up spinner button to the right of the **Lag** box to increase the lag time to **2d** (i.e. two days).

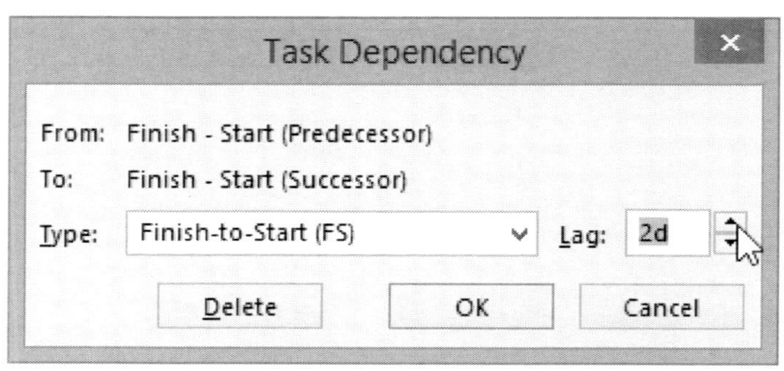

4. Click **OK** and notice the effect. The start of task **2** is delayed by two days.

Driving Lesson 50 - Continued

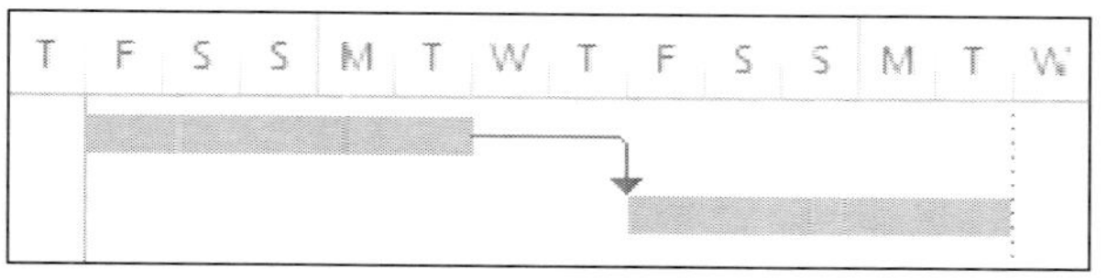

Adding lag time often extends a project's duration.

5. Using the same technique, add a lag time of two days to task **8** (this is linked to task **7** with a **Start-to-Start** dependency).

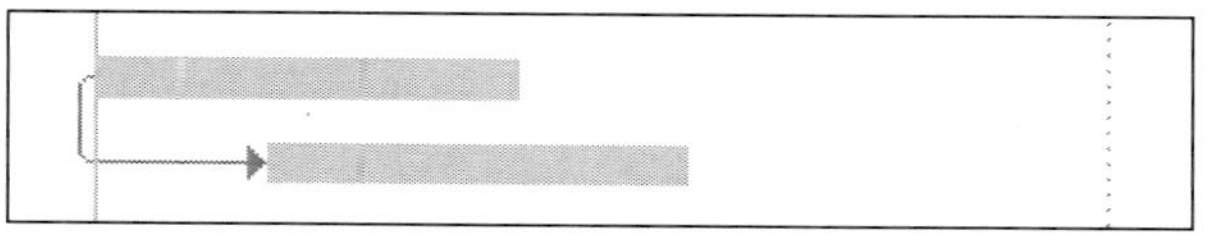

6. Next, select task **14** and open the **Task Information** dialog box. Display the **Predecessors** tab and notice that this task is linked to task **13** with a **Finish-to-Finish** dependency.

7. Click once in the **Lag** box for this link and change the value to **2d**.

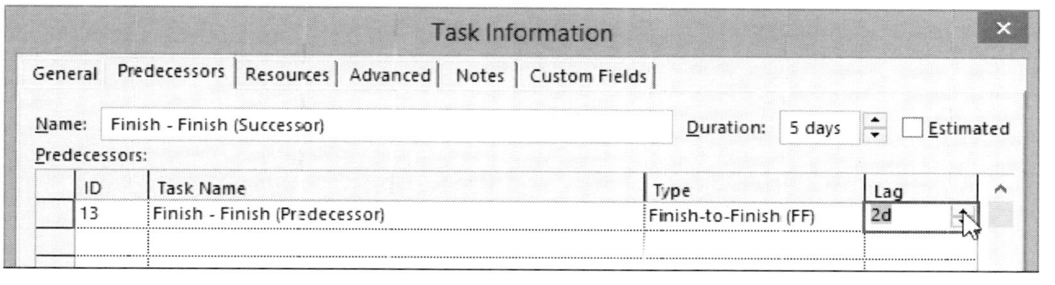

8. Click **OK** and notice the effect. This is another way to add lag to a task.

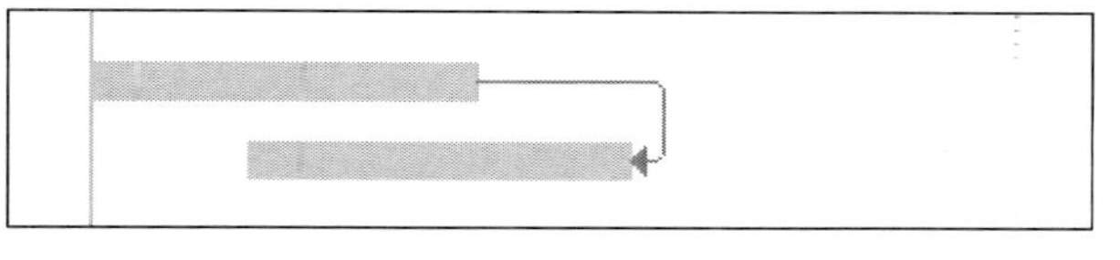

9. Using whichever technique you prefer, add a two day lag between tasks **19** and **20**. These are linked with a **Start-to-Finish** dependency.

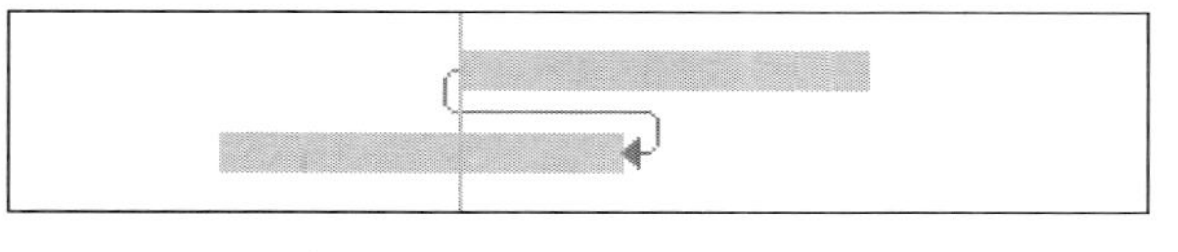

10. You have now added lag time to each type of task dependency. Consider the effect of doing this and notice how each effects successor start dates.

*To update or delete a task's lag time, simply change the value in either the **Task Dependency** or **Task Information** dialog boxes. **0d** will remove lag.*

11. Save the project as **lag time** and leave it open for the next lesson.

Driving Lesson 51 - Lead Time

Park and Read

You may find that you want to start a task before its predecessor has completely finished. To do this, you can add **lead time** to the task so it begins earlier than scheduled.

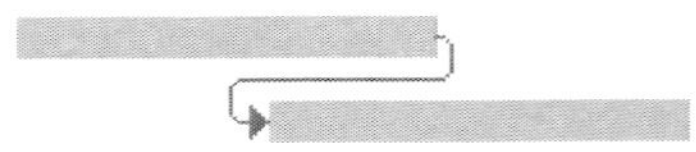

For example, on a house building project, it makes sense to paint the walls first and then install the carpets. However, if the painting task includes two days to allow the paint to dry, you can add a two-day lead time to the *carpeting* task so it can start a little ahead of schedule.

Manoeuvres

1. Let's now add a two-day lead time between the second pairing of each dependency type. Double-click the link between tasks **4** and **5** on the **Gantt Chart**. The **Task Dependency** dialog box appears.

Lead time is entered as negative lag time (i.e. ***-2d****). It can be entered, edited or removed on the* ***Task Dependency*** *or* ***Task Information*** *dialog boxes.*

2. To demonstrate the effect lead time has on a **Finish-to-Start** link, change the **Lag** value to **-2d** using the down spinner button.

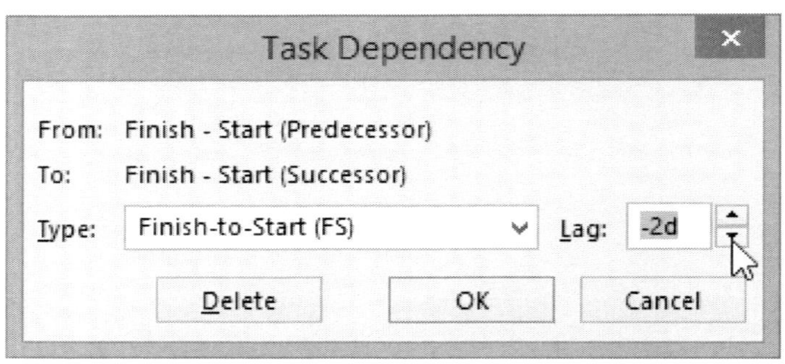

3. Click **OK**. Task **5** now starts two days before task **4** finishes.
4. Add a two day lead between tasks **10** and **11** (**Start-to-Start**). This will move task **11** before the start of the project. Of course, tasks shouldn't start before the project begins, but for demonstration purposes click **OK**.
5. Add a two day lead between tasks **16** and **17** and tasks **22** and **23**.
6. Save the project as **lead time** and close it.

You can also add lag and lead time as a percentage value rather than a duration (e.g. ***80%*** *- a task will not start until its predecessor is 80% complete).*

Driving Lesson 52 - Elapsed Time

Park and Read

Not all tasks should be restricted by a project's working time settings; some simply take a fixed amount of time to complete. For example, allowing concrete to dry might take five days, but this time is not confined to an 8-hour working day – it will happen all on its own at night and during weekends.

To remove a task from a project's working time, you can assign it an **elapsed** duration. It will then run 24 hours a day, 7 days a week, regardless of weekends, holidays and non-working time.

To make a task use elapsed time, simply add **e** before the unit of time required in the **Duration** cell. For example, **5ed** would be five elapsed days, **3ew** would be three elapsed weeks, and so on.

Manoeuvres

1. Open the project **Fence**. This incomplete project plan was created to help organise the building of a new garden fence.

The person building the fence can only work weekends. As a result, notice that the project's working time only includes Saturdays and Sundays.

2. Locate task **11**, **Drying time**. It takes five days for poured concrete to dry, so enter **5d** in the **Duration** cell.

11		Drying time	5 days

3. The project plan currently waits until the next available working day to start task **11** – fives days after task **10** has finished! As the concrete starts drying immediately after it is poured, this doesn't make much sense.

4. In the **Duration** cell for task **11**, enter **5ed** instead and press <**Enter**>.

11		Drying time	5 edays

5. This makes task **11** use elapsed time – which ignores non-working time – and so it starts immediately after its predecessor has finished.

6. Enter **5ed** in the **Duration** field for task **15** also.

7. Change the duration for task **17** so that it uses elapsed time too. The project should now be completed on **05/07/2018**.

Elapsed time can be used to help reduce task durations. As you will see later, the sooner a project is completed, the sooner it will stop incurring costs.

8. Save the project as **elapsed time** and close it.

Driving Lesson 53 - Develop Your Skills

Park and Read

In this lesson you will add more detail to the **movie** project plan.

Manoeuvres

1. Open the project **movie** that you created earlier.

*An up-to-date model copy of the **movie** project is available in the data files folder **Training**. This is named **section7 movie**. If you would like to use this, open the project and save it as **movie** in the main data files folder.*

2. It would be a good idea to leave two days between tasks **5** and **6**. Select task **6**, **First review** on the **Task List** and open the **Task Information** dialog box.

3. On the **Predecessors** tab, set a **Lag** of **2d** between this task and its predecessor, task **5**.

ID	Task Name	Type	Lag
5	First draft	Finish-to-Start (FS)	2d

4. Click **OK** and notice the effect.

5. Add a two day lag between task **8** and task **7** also.

6. Double-click the link on the **Gantt Chart** between tasks **16** and **17**. Then use the **Task Dependency** dialog box to add a **Lag** of **2d**. Click **OK**.

*It doesn't matter if you use the **Task Information** or **Task Dependency** dialog box to add lag or lead time.*

7. Next, select task **23**, **Hire technicians**. This task can start five days before task **21**, **Erect set** has completed.

8. Display the **Task Information** dialog box. On the **Predecessors** tab, set a **Lag** of **-5d** between this task and its predecessor, task **21**.

	Type	Lag
	Finish-to-Start (FS)	-5d

9. Click **OK** and notice the effect. As a negative lag was entered, this creates a lead time of three days.

*Notice how tasks **24** and **25** also start early as they are linked to task **23** with a dependency type of **Start-to-Start**.*

10. Save the project and close it.

Driving Lesson 54 - Revision

Park and Read

At the end of every section you get the chance to complete one or more revision exercises to develop your skills and prepare you for your ECDL certification test. You should aim to complete the following steps without referring back to the previous lessons.

Manoeuvres

1. Open the project **revision** that you created earlier.

*An up-to-date model copy of the **revision** project is available in the data files folder **Training**. This is named **section7 revision**. If you would like to use this, open the project and save it as **revision** in the main data files folder.*

2. Examine tasks **3** and **4**. You would like a four day break between these tasks, so add a four day lag to task **4**.
3. You would also like a delay of one day between tasks **4** and **5**, so add a one day lag to task **5**.
4. Examine tasks **14** and **15**. The decorators and fitters can start two days before the builders have completed their work (they can work in the areas that the builders have completed). Add in a two day lead to task **14**.

*As task **15** is linked to task **14** with a **Start-to-Start** dependency, it also benefits from task **14's** increased lead time.*

5. You would also like to give task **19** a one day head-start, so add a one day lead to task **19**.
6. You've changed you mind and only want a two day lag before task **4** starts. Make this change.
7. Save the project.

*A sample project named **section7 revision complete** can be found in the **Revisions** folder within the data files. You can use this to compare your work against a model solution.*

8. Close all open files but leave *Project* open for the next section.

*Now complete the **Record of Achievement Matrix** at the back of the guide. You should only move on when confident with the topics and features described in this section.*

Section 8 Constraints & Deadlines

By the end of this section you should be able to:

Understand task constraints

Recognise fixed and variable constraints

Add and delete constraints

Understand deadlines

Create and delete deadlines

Work through the **Driving Lessons** in this section to gain an understanding of the above features.

For each **Driving Lesson**, read all of the **Park and Read** instructions and then, if applicable, perform the numbered steps of the **Manoeuvres**. Complete the **Revision** exercise(s) at the end of the section to test your knowledge.

Driving Lesson 55 - Task Constraints

Park and Read

When you create an auto-scheduled task in *Project*, it is usually set to occur **As Soon As Possible** (i.e. at the start of the project).

However, tasks often need to begin or end on a specific date (or must start on or finish no later than a specific date). These dates are known as **constraints** as they limit when the task can occur. Constraints include:

As Late As Possible	A task scheduled to start as late as possible
As Soon As Possible	A task scheduled to start as early as possible
Finish No Earlier Than	A task will never finish earlier than this date
Finish No Later Than	A task will never finish later than this date
Must Finish On	A task will always finish on this date
Must Start On	A task will always start on this date
Start No Earlier Than	A task will never start earlier than this date
Start No Later Than	A task will never start later than this date

It is always best to allow Project *to automatically schedule your tasks. Because of this, it is best to use constraints only when they are absolutely necessary.*

Manoeuvres

1. Open the project **House**. This is a simple plan for a house building project with a number of **Finish-to-Start** and **Start-to-Start** dependencies.

2. Display the **VIEW** tab and click the **Zoom Entire Project** button in the **Zoom** group. The entire **Gantt Chart** can now be seen.

3. The project is scheduled to start on **01/01/2018**. This can be seen on the **Gantt Chart** and **Timescale**.

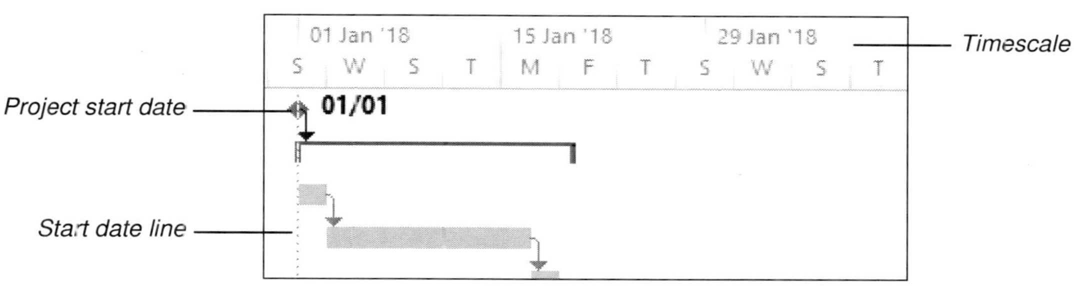

*Notice the dotted **Start date line** on the **Gantt Chart**. This indicates the start date of the project.*

4. At the moment, the auto-scheduled **Finish date** is **12/03/2018**. This is also shown on the **Gantt Chart**.

Driving Lesson 55 - Continued

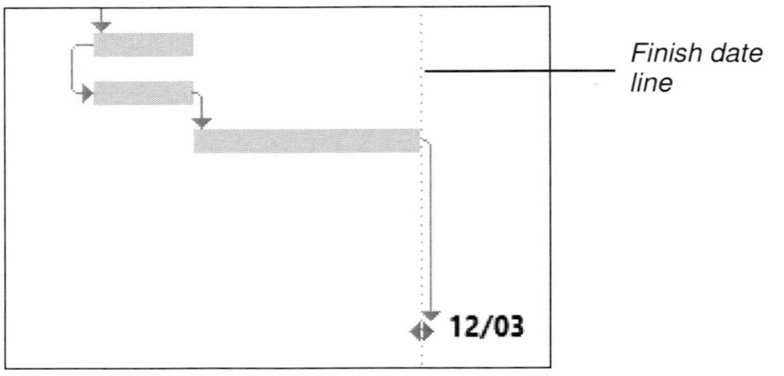

5. Select task **19**, **Landscaping** in the **Task List**. You need to start this task as late as possible during the project. Open the **Task Information** dialog box and display the **Advanced** tab.

*Notice that the task is auto-scheduled to occur **As Soon As Possible**.*

6. Click the **Constraint type** drop-down button and examine the options that appear. Consider how each could be used to constrain tasks.

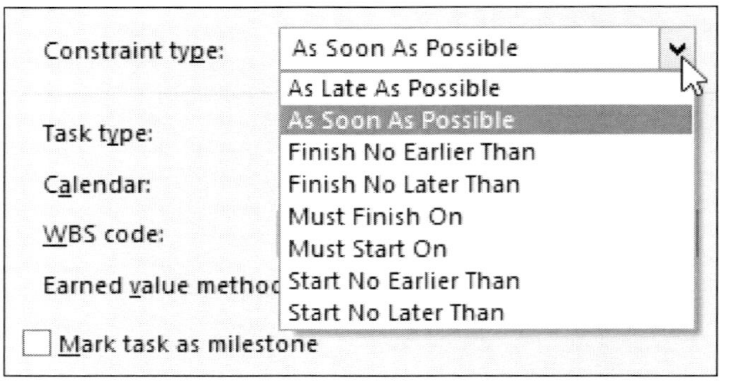

7. Select **As Late As Possible** and click **OK**. Task **19** now starts as late as possible in the project. Its end date is **12/03/2018**.

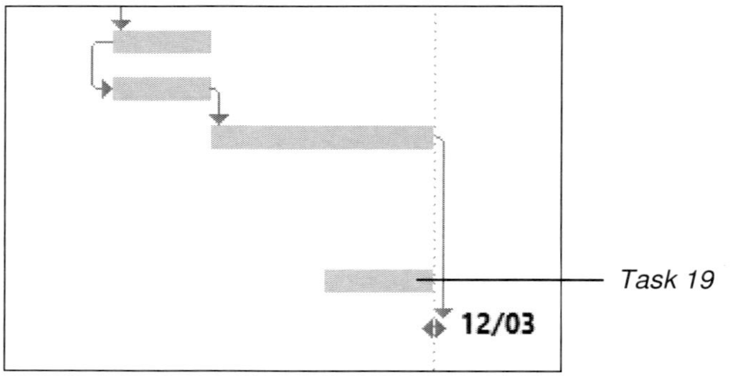

*If you schedule from a project's finish date rather than its start date (by selecting **Project Finish Date** in **Schedule from** on the **Project Information** dialog box), auto-scheduled tasks will occur **As Late As Possible** by default.*

8. Save the project as **constraints** and leave it open for the next lesson.

Driving Lesson 56 - Fixed Constraints

Park and Read

As you have already seen, the task constraints **As Late As Possible** and **As Soon As Possible** do not require specific dates. *Project* will automatically use dependencies and durations to schedule these types of task for you.

However, you can also create fixed constraints which specify exactly when tasks should start or finish. This means that they will occur at a specific time in the schedule, regardless of other task dependencies.

Manoeuvres

1. Select task **17, Land registry**, which refers to the paperwork that must be submitted to the government when building a house.
2. Open the **Task Information** dialog box and display the **Advanced** tab. Click the **Constraint type** drop-down box and select **Must Finish On**.
3. Then, click once in the **Constraint date** box and enter **01/02/2018**.

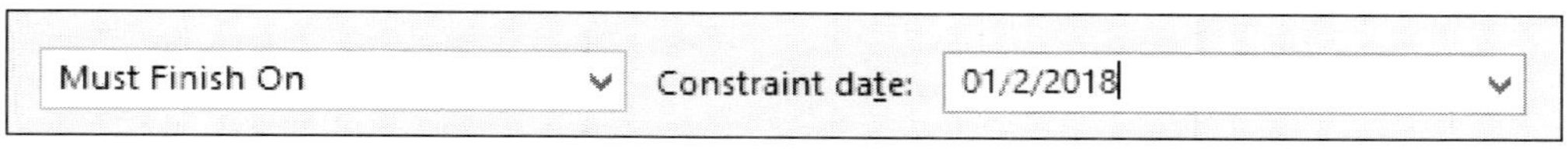

*You could also click the drop-down arrow on the **Constraint date** box and use the calendar to navigate to and select* February 01, 2018.

4. Click **OK**. Task **17** is now forced to *finish* on February 01, 2018.

*Notice that a constraint icon, ▦, has appeared in the **Indicators** column to show there is a constraint for this task. Move the mouse over the icon to see it.*

5. Increase the **Duration** of task **17** to **10** days – it still finishes on the date specified (the start date is brought forward instead).
6. With task **17** selected, change the constraint type to **Must Start On**. Leave the **Constraint date** as **Thu 01/02/18** and click **OK**.
7. The task is now forced to *start* on February 01, 2018. Decrease the **Duration** of task **17** to **5** days – it still starts on the date specified.
8. You have been informed that you need to *finish* submitting the land registry documentation on *Monday, January 22, 2018*. Change the constraint for task **17** accordingly.

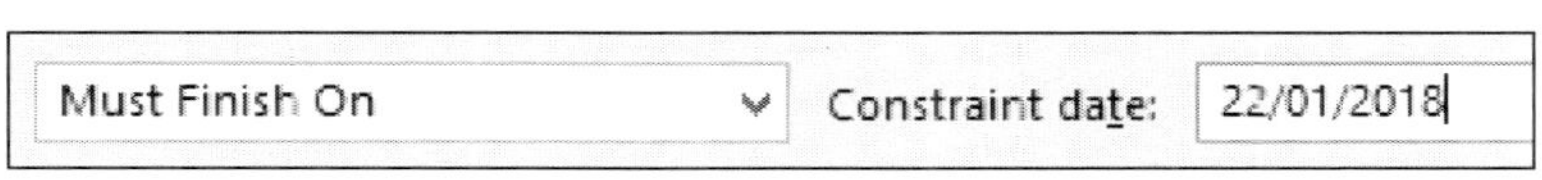

9. Save the project and leave it open for the next lesson.

Driving Lesson 57 - Flexible Constraints

Park and Read

Flexible constraints allow you to specify the date on which tasks must have started or finished by. *Project* is free to automatically schedule these types of task as normal so long as the constraint is met.

Manoeuvres

1. Before the house is built, you need to apply for a council tax band. Select task **18, Tax band**.
2. Open the **Task Information** dialog box and display the **Advanced** tab. Click the **Constraint type** drop-down box and select **Finish No Earlier Than**.
3. Then, click once in the **Constraint date** box and enter **19/02/2018**.

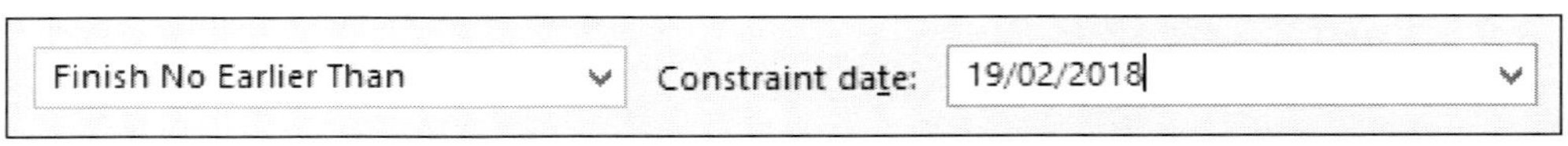

4. Click **OK**.
5. Task **18** is now forced to *finish* no earlier than February 19, 2018. However, *Project* is free to automatically schedule the task so that it finishes later than that date.
6. Increase the **Duration** of task **18** to **10** days – it still finishes on the date specified (the start date is brought forward instead).
7. Change the constraint for task **18** to **Finish No Later Than**. Leave the **Constraint date** as **Mon 19/02/18** and click **OK**. Task **18** is now free to be auto-scheduled by *Project* so long as its finish date is before February 19, 2018.
8. You have been informed that you need to start applying for a tax band no earlier than *Monday, January 29, 2018*. Change the constraint for task **18** to **Start No Earlier Than**.
9. Then, click once in the **Constraint date** box and enter **29/01/2018**.

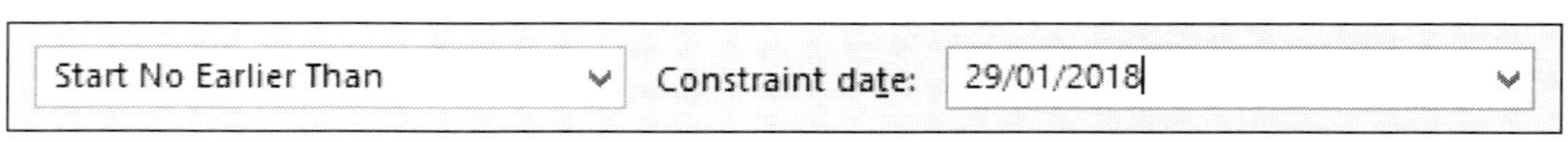

10. Click **OK**. The task is now forced to *start* no earlier than January 29, 2018. Decrease the **Duration** of task **18** to **5** days – it still starts on the date specified.
11. Save the project and leave it open for the next lesson.

Driving Lesson 58 - Schedule Conflicts

Park and Read

Scheduling conflicts can occur when you try to add constraints to linked tasks that don't make sense. For example, if two tasks are linked with a **Finish-to-Start** dependency, a schedule conflict will occur if you try to force the successor task to start before the predecessor has finished.

Manoeuvres

1. Select task **8**, **Ground works**. Then set a **Constraint type** of **Must Start On** and a **Constraint date** of **29/01/2018**.
2. Click **OK** and a **Planning Wizard** dialog box appears.

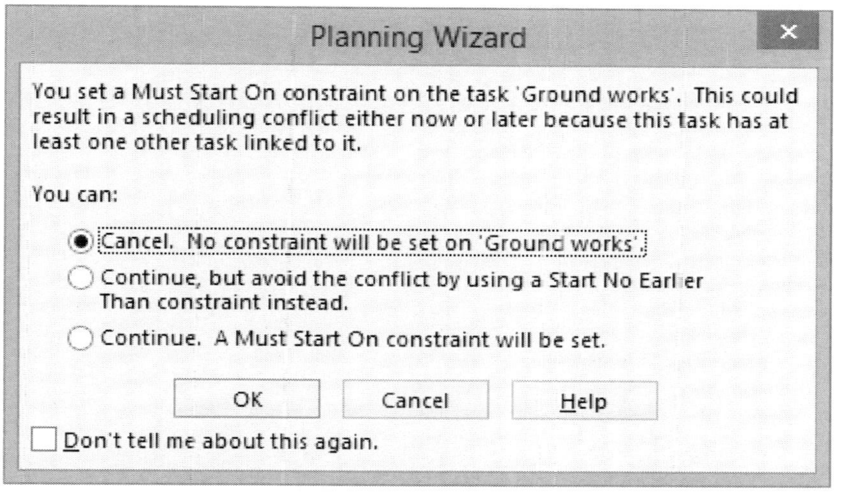

3. Read the text on the dialog box and select **Continue. A Must Start On constraint will be set**.
4. Click **OK** and notice the effect. Task **8** is forced to start on January 29, 2018.

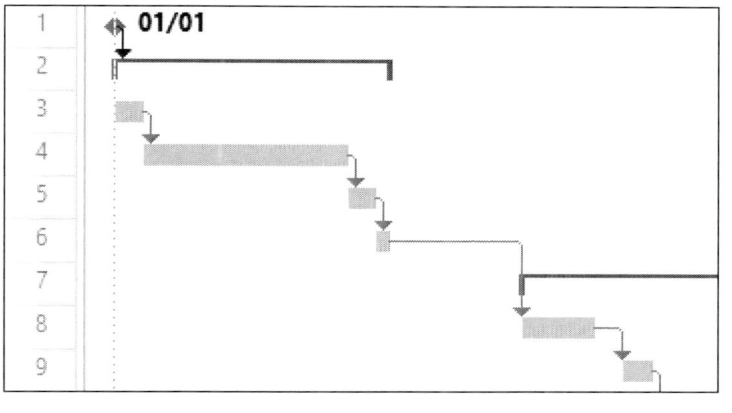

5. Increase the **Duration** of task **4** to **15** days. Notice that the start date of tasks **5** and **6** are pushed back, filling the space before task **8** starts.

Driving Lesson 58 - Continued

6. Now increase the **Duration** of task **4** to **20** days. A scheduling conflict occurs and a **Planning Wizard** dialog box appears.

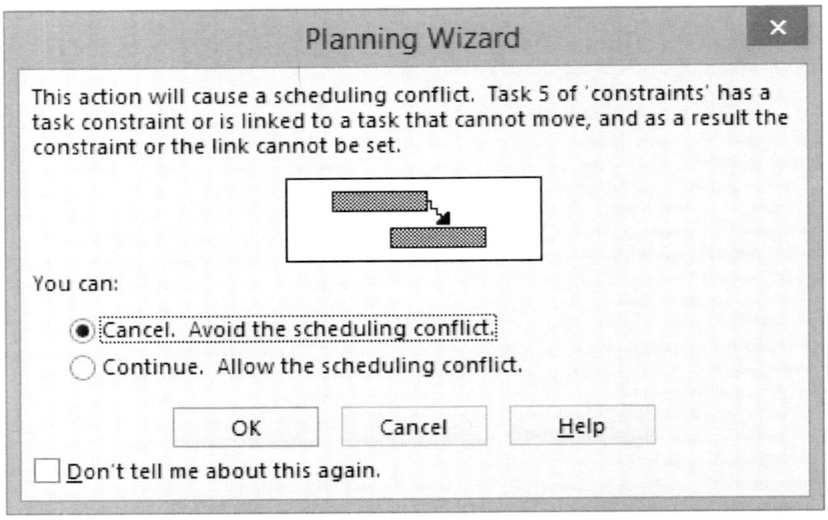

7. Select **Continue. Allow the scheduling conflict** and then click **OK**.

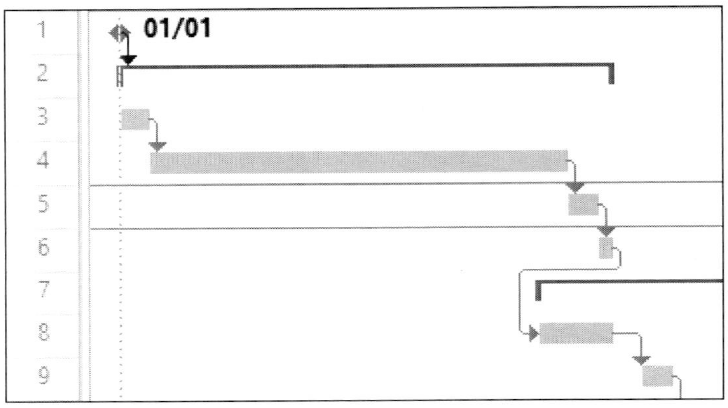

8. Notice the scheduling conflict that has occurred. Task **8** now starts before tasks **4**, **5** and **6** have finished. As task **8** is linked by a **Finish-to-Start** dependency with task **6**, this is not possible.

*To remove a constraint, simply set its value back to **As Soon As Possible**.*

9. Open the **Task Information** dialog box for task **8** and display the **Advanced** tab.

*You can double-click the constraint icon, ▦, in the **Indicators** column to show the **Task Information** dialog box.*

10. Set the **Constraint type** to **As Soon As Possible** and click **OK**. The constraint is removed and *Project* automatically corrects the scheduling conflict.

11. Save the project and leave it open for the next exercise.

Driving Lesson 59 - Deadlines

Park and Read

A deadline is simply a target date that allows you to track when a task should finish. It does not affect your schedule and will not fix a task's start or end date like a constraint.

*If a task's deadline passes and the task has not yet finished, an indicator, ◆, will appear in the **Indicators** column.*

Manoeuvres

1. Select task **20**, **Project finish**. You have been informed that the whole project must be finished by March 14, 2018. Let's enter this as a deadline.
2. Open the **Task Information** dialog box and display the **Advanced** tab. Then, enter **14/03/2018** in the **Deadline** box.

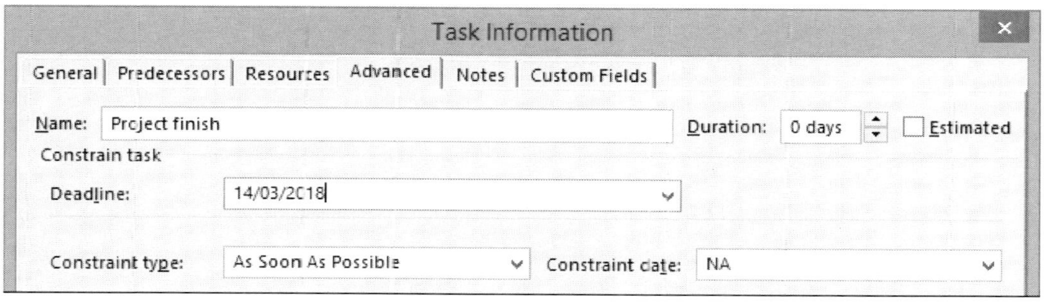

*The drop-down arrow on the **Deadline** box can be used to display a calendar.*

3. Click **OK**. A green arrow icon, ⬇, appears on the **Gantt Chart** which shows this task's deadline date.
4. Task **20** is a milestone that currently finishes on **26/03/2018**. Notice the deadline indicator, ◆, in the **Indicators** column that shows that this task's deadline has been missed.
5. Decrease the **Duration** of task **4** to **10 days**. This reduces the overall time taken to complete the project and now task **20** meets its deadline.
6. Select task **20**, **Project finish** and display the **Task Information** dialog box. On the **Advanced** tab, delete the date in the **Deadline** box and click **OK**. The deadline is removed.
7. Set a new deadline for task **8**, **Ground works**. Set the deadline date as **29/01/2018**. Will task **8** meet its deadline?
8. Change the **Duration** of task **5** to **10 days**. Does task **8** still meet its deadline?
9. Save the project and close it.

Driving Lesson 60 - Develop Your Skills

Park and Read

In this lesson you will add more detail to the **movie** project plan.

Manoeuvres

1. Open the project **movie** that you created earlier.

*An up-to-date model copy of the **movie** project is available in the data files folder **Training**. This is named **section8 movie**. If you would like to use this, open the project and save it as **movie** in the main data files folder.*

2. Insert the three following tasks <u>above</u> task **28**, **Release movie**:

Safety assessment	**30 days**
Release forms	**5 days**
Taxes	**3 days**

3. Select task **28**, **Safety assessment**. A health and safety inspection will start on March 10, 2017. Open the **Task Information** dialog box and display the **Advanced** tab.
4. Set a **Constraint type** of **Must Start On** and enter a **Constraint date** of **10/03/2017**. Click **OK** and observe the result.
5. Next, select task **29**, **Release forms**. This task needs to occur as late in the project as possible. Use the **Task Information** dialog box to select a **Constraint type** of **As Late As Possible**.
6. Click **OK** and observe the result.
7. Next, select task **30**, **Taxes**. For this project, tax forms need to be submitted on April 5, 2017.
8. Using the **Task Information** dialog box, set a **Constraint type** of **Must Finish On** and enter a **Constraint date** of **05/04/2017**.
9. The movie needs to be completed by June 15, 2017. Let's enter this as a deadline. Select task **32**, **Movie complete**.
10. Using the **Task Information** dialog box, enter a new deadline of **15/06/2017** in the **Deadline** box.
11. Click **OK** to apply the changes and notice the deadline icon, ⇩, that appears on the **Gantt Chart**. Will the current schedule meet the project's deadline?
12. Save the project and close it.

Driving Lesson 61 - Revision

Park and Read

At the end of every section you get the chance to complete one or more revision exercises to develop your skills and prepare you for your ECDL certification test. You should aim to complete the following steps without referring back to the previous lessons.

Manoeuvres

1. Open the project **revision** that you created earlier.

*An up-to-date model copy of the **revision** project is available in the data files folder **Training**. This is named **section8 revision**. If you would like to use this, open the project and save it as **revision** in the main data files folder.*

2. Insert a new task above task **28**, **Move complete**. Name it **Finalise bills** and give it a **Duration** of **2 days**. Make sure it is a level 1 task (not a subtask of task **23**).
3. Task **28**, **Finalise bills** currently occurs as early in the project as possible. Add a constraint so it occurs as *late* as possible instead.
4. Insert a new task above task **29**, **Move complete**. Name it **Customer notice** and give it a **Duration** of **5 days**.
5. You are planning to send letters to customers to inform them of the office's new address. To do this, you have organised a special deal with your local mail delivery company. However, this offer is only valid for five days starting October 2, 2017. Add a constraint to task **29**, **Customer notice** so that it **Must Start On 02/10/17**.
6. Task **30**, **Move complete**, should be completed by *October 30, 2017*. Create a deadline to record this target date.
7. Your manager asks you not to start tasks **9** and **10** any earlier than **20/09/2017**. Add an appropriate **Start No Earlier Than** constraint for task **9** to do this (this will also change the start date for task **10** as it is linked to task **9** with a **Start-to-Start** dependency).
8. Save the project and close any open files.

*A sample project named **section8 revision complete** can be found in the **Revisions** folder within the data files. You can use this to compare your work against a model solution.*

*Now complete the **Record of Achievement Matrix** at the back of the guide. You should only move on when confident with the topics and features described in this section.*

Section 9
Resources & Costs

By the end of this section you should be able to:

Understand resources

Create and assign resources

Understand project costs

Apply costs to tasks

Recognise effort-driven scheduling

Work through the **Driving Lessons** in this section to gain an understanding of the above features.

For each **Driving Lesson**, read all of the **Park and Read** instructions and then, if applicable, perform the numbered steps of the **Manoeuvres**. Complete the **Revision** exercise(s) at the end of the section to test your knowledge.

Driving Lesson 62 - Creating Resources

Park and Read

Resources are the people, materials and equipment needed to complete a project. You can create three different types of resource:

Work	The people and machinery that perform a task
Material	Any materials or consumable supplies used by a task
Cost	General costs such as legal fees or travel expenses

After producing a work breakdown structure (i.e. a list of tasks), the next step is to create and assign resources.

Manoeuvres

1. Open the project **Event**. This simple project plan was developed to help organise the creation and running of a garden party.

2. Display the **VIEW** tab and click the **Resource Sheet** button in the **Resource Views** group (click the button's icon, not the drop-down arrow).

3. The project's resource sheet appears. All of the resources that are available to the project can be entered here. A number of resources have already been entered to save time.

Resource Name	Type	Material	Init	Group	Max.	Std. Rate	Ovt.	Cost/Use	Accrue At	Base
Atesh	Work		A	Construction	100%	£20.00/hr	£0.00/hr	£0.00	Prorated	Standard
Jean	Work		J	Construction	100%	£25.00/hr	£0.00/hr	£0.00	Prorated	Standard
Zak	Work		Z	Cook	100%	£10.00/hr	£15.00/hr	£0.00	Prorated	Standard
Priti	Work		P	Waiter	100%	£11.00/hr	£0.00/hr	£0.00	Prorated	Standard
Hiro	Work		H	Waiter	100%	£11.00/hr	£0.00/hr	£0.00	Prorated	Standard
Kerry	Work		K	Cleaner	100%	£0.00/hr	£0.00/hr	£0.00	Prorated	Standard
Bob	Work		B	Cleaner	100%	£0.00/hr	£0.00/hr	£0.00	Prorated	Standard
Cooker	Work		C	Equipment	100%	£0.00/hr	£0.00/hr	£0.00	Prorated	Standard
Starter	Material		FS			£8.00		£0.00	Prorated	
Main	Material		FM			£14.00		£0.00	Prorated	
Dessert	Material		FD			£8.00		£0.00	Prorated	
Tent	Cost		T						Prorated	

*If the **Resource Sheet** does not appear as shown above, make sure **Entry** is selected on the **Tables** drop-down button (in the **Data** group on the **VIEW** tab).*

4. *Darren* is a photographer who will work on the project. Let's create a new **Work** resource for him. Click once in the **Resource Name** field for empty row **9**. Enter **Darren** and press <**Enter**>.

Resources can be placed in groups to make them easier to find and sort (which you will see later).

5. In the **Group** column for row **9**, enter **Photographer**.

Driving Lesson 62 - Continued

9		Darren	Work		D	Photographer

*The **Max. Units** column can be used to specify how much of a resource is available for use – this is known as its **capacity**. For example, if a work resource's **Max. Units** value is 50%, that person will only be available for 50% of the working day. This is useful for part-time workers.*

6. Cleaners require cleaning materials to wash up after guests have finished their meals. Let's create a new **Material** resource. Click once in the **Resource Name** field for empty row **13**, enter **Washing up liquid** and press <**Enter**>.

7. Click once in the **Type** column for row **13**. Then, use the drop-down button, , that appears to change this resource's type to **Material**.

*Material resources can come in different types of **unit**. For example, bricks on a building project may be used in tonnes, so one tonne of bricks can be considered one "unit". These simple units of measurement can be entered in the **Material Label** column.*

8. Click once in the **Material Label** column for row **13**. Enter **bottles** and press <**Enter**>.

13		Washing up liquid	Material	bottles	W	

Cost resources can be used to add specific costs to a project that don't have any connection to work or materials.

9. Let's create a new **Cost** resource. Click once in the **Resource Name** field for empty row **15**, enter **Site fees** and press <**Enter**>.

10. Complete the resource as shown below.

15		Site fees	Cost		S	

*The **Base** column can be used to select different working times for different resources (as seen in lesson 8).*

11. You will work with these resources in the lessons that follow. For now, save the project as **party** and leave it open for the next lesson.

Driving Lesson 63 - Costs

Park and Read

Most resources cost money to use. For example, you will need to pay a person an hourly wage for their time, or pay a company a fee to hire their equipment. These costs can be added on the **Resource Sheet**.

As you will learn later, it is very important that a project is completed "on budget" (i.e. you don't spend more money than you have). By entering resource costs, you can use Project *to control and manage your budget.*

Importantly, costs assigned to work and material resources are called **variable** costs because they can change depending on how much of them you use (e.g. the cost to use a work resource will depend on how many hours you use it for). Cost resources, however, do not change and are known as **fixed** costs.

Manoeuvres

1. With the **party** project still open from the previous lesson, examine the **Std. Rate** column. This can be used to enter the cost of a resource.

*If the resource is a person, the value in the **Std. Rate** column is that person's wage; if a piece of equipment or material, it is its hourly cost to use.*

2. Select the **Std. Rate** cell for resource **6**, **Kerry**. *Kerry* is a cleaner who works for £8 per hour, so type **8** and press <**Enter**>.

K	Cleaner	100%	£8.00/hr	£0.00/hr	£0.00

3. In the **Ovt. Rate** cell for resource **6**, enter **15** to specify *Kerry's* hourly overtime rate and press <**Enter**>.

K	Cleaner	100%	£8.00/hr	£15.00/hr	£0.00

*A person's overtime rate is the amount of pay earned <u>after</u> working a standard full day's work (as specified in the **Change Working Time** dialog box).*

4. Enter the following cost details for resource **7**, **Bob**:

B	Cleaner	100%	£10.00/hr	£17.00/hr	£0.00

*The **Std. Rate** column can be used to specify how much it costs to use a resource over time (e.g. its cost per hour or day). However, some resources simply cost a fixed amount whenever you use them. If this is the case, that amount can be entered in the **Cost/Use** column.*

Driving Lesson 63 - Continued

5. Rather than get paid by the hour, *Darren* charges a flat fee of £300 to take photos at a garden party. In the **Cost/Use** cell for resource **9**, type **300** and press <**Enter**>.

D	Photographer	100%	£0.00/hr	£0.00/hr	£300.00

*An hourly rate is the default unit of cost for a **Work** resource. You can also use the abbreviations shown in lesson 20 to enter rates per day (/**d**), per week (/**w**) or per month (/**m**).*

6. Locate resource **8**, **Cooker**. Although this is a piece of equipment rather than a person, it is still a productive resource. It costs £90 per day to hire, so enter **90/d** in this resource's **Std Rate** cell.

Cooker	Work	C	Equipment	100%	£90.00/day

7. Locate resource **13**, **Washing up liquid**. Each bottle of washing up liquid costs £5, so enter **5** in this resource's **Std Rate** cell.

Washing up liquid	Material	bottles	W			£5.00

8. You have now completed the **Resource Sheet** for this project. Save the project and leave it open for the next lesson.

*Why not set a rate for **Cost** resources? Think of these as general charges that may apply at different rates if used multiple times during the project (e.g. train tickets). The actual costs for these are entered manually when assigning the resource to a task.*

Driving Lesson 64 - Assigning Work Resources

Park and Read

Once you have created a number of resources, you can then start assigning them to your tasks. This allows you to plan and cost the "effort" (work required) to complete your project.

It is important to realise that there is a relationship between a task's duration and the resources needed to complete it. For example, if you increase the number of workers on a task, you should decrease its duration (and vice-versa).

Manoeuvres

1. With the **party** project still open from the previous lesson, display the **VIEW** tab and click the **Gantt Chart** button in the **Task Views** group (click the button's icon, not the drop-down arrow).

*You can also move quickly between views using the view buttons on the right of the **Status Bar**. Click to view the **Gantt Chart** and to view the **Resource Sheet**.*

2. Select task **7**, **Set up tent**. You need to assign construction workers to this task, so display the **RESOURCE** tab and click **Assign Resources**.

3. The **Assign Resources** dialog box appears. This lists all of the resources created on the **Resource Sheet**. Click **Atesh** and then click **Assign**.

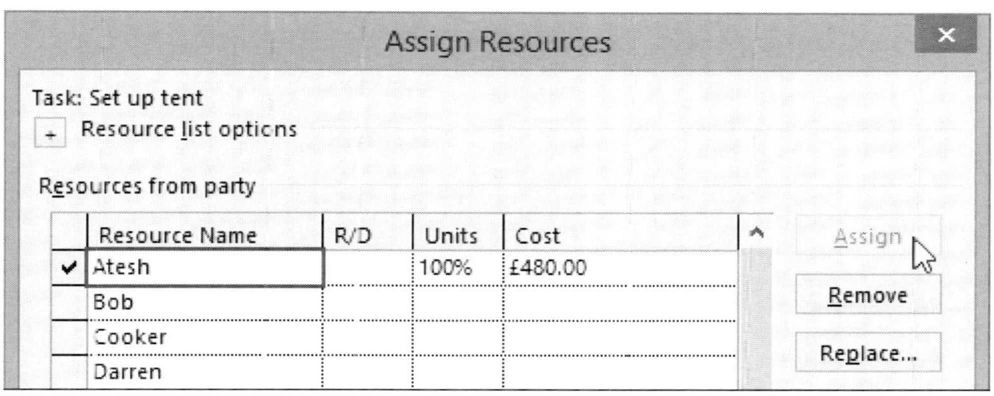

4. *Atesh* is now assigned to task **7**. Notice the **Cost** value that appears – this is automatically calculated based on the duration of the task and *Atesh's* hourly rate.

5. Click **Close** and notice the change on the **Gantt Chart**. The resource name appears to the right of the task's bar.

More than one work resource can be assigned to a task.

Driving Lesson 64 - Continued

6. With task **7** still selected, display the **Assign Resources** dialog box again.

7. Scroll down and click once on **Jean**. Then click **Assign** again. There are now two workers assigned to this task.

	Resource Name	R/D	Units	Cost
✔	Atesh		100%	£480.00
✔	Jean		100%	£600.00

*The **Cost** values are different between resources as* Jean *is paid a higher hourly rate than* Atesh*.*

8. Click **Close** and notice the changes on the **Gantt Chart**. The resource names appear to the right of the task's bar.

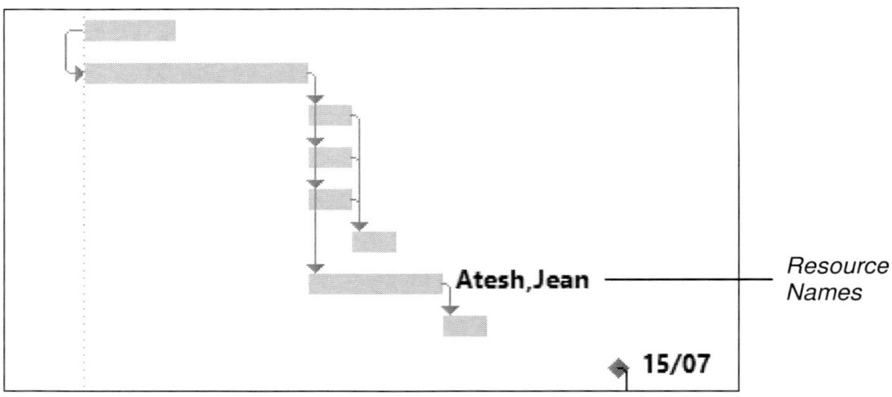

9. Next, select task **8**. Then click the **Assign Resources** button and assign **Atesh** and **Jean** again.

*You do not need to close the **Assign Resources** dialog box. You can leave it open and select another task in the **Task List**.*

10. Carefully assign the following resources:

    Assign **Cooker** and **Priti** to task **10**
    Assign **Hiro** and **Priti** to tasks **13**, **14** and **15**
    Assign **Darren** to task **16**
    Assign **Atesh** and **Jean** to tasks **18** and **19**
    Assign **Kerry** and **Bob** to task **20**

*You can select more than one task at a time in the **Task List** and assign resources to them in one go.*

11. Close the **Assign Resources** dialog box for now.

12. Save the project and leave it open for the next lesson.

Driving Lesson 65 - Assigning Materials/Costs

Park and Read

Material and cost resources can be assigned to tasks in the same way as work resources. However, a material resource's quantity (or units), and cost resource's fixed price, can also be entered.

Manoeuvres

1. You estimate that there will be 80 people attending the garden party. 60 will want a starter (first course), 80 will want a main (second course), and 30 will want a dessert (third course). Let's add these material resources...

2. Select task **13** and open the **Assign Resources** dialog box. Then find and select **Starter** and click **Assign**. Notice that only **1** unit is assigned.

3. Click once in the **Units** cell for **Starter**. Type **60** and press <**Enter**>.

	Resource Name	R/D	Units	Cost
✔	Hiro		100%	£11.00
✔	Priti		100%	£11.00
✔	Starter		60	£480.00

4. Notice that the **Cost** has increased. **Close** the **Assign Resources** dialog box and notice the effect on the **Gantt Chart**.

5. Next, use the **Assign Resources** dialog box again to assign **80** mains to task **14**.

	Resource Name	R/D	Units	Cost
✔	Hiro		100%	£11.00
✔	Main		80	£1,120.00
✔	Priti		100%	£11.00

6. Assign **30** desserts to task **15**.

	Resource Name	R/D	Units	Cost
✔	Dessert		30	£240.00

7. Finally, assign **10 bottles** of washing up liquid to task **20**.

	Resource Name	R/D	Units	Cost
✔	Washing up liquid		10 bottles	£50.00

*Notice that the material labels appear on the **Gantt Chart**.*

8. You have confirmed that the cost for hiring a tent for the garden party is a fixed fee of £999. Let's enter this into your plan...

9. Select task **5**, **Hire tent**, and assign the cost resource **Tent**.

Driving Lesson 65 - Continued

10. Then, click once in the **Cost** cell (currently containing the value **£0.00**) and replace this with **999**. Press <**Enter**> to confirm the change.

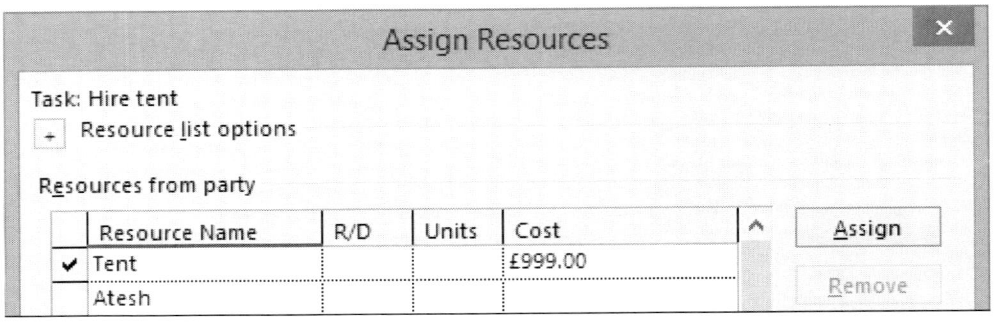

11. Finally, assign the cost resource **Site fees** to task **7**, **Set up tent**. You have learned that the fees will cost **£300**.

12. You have now assigned resources to this project. Close the **Assign Resources** box.

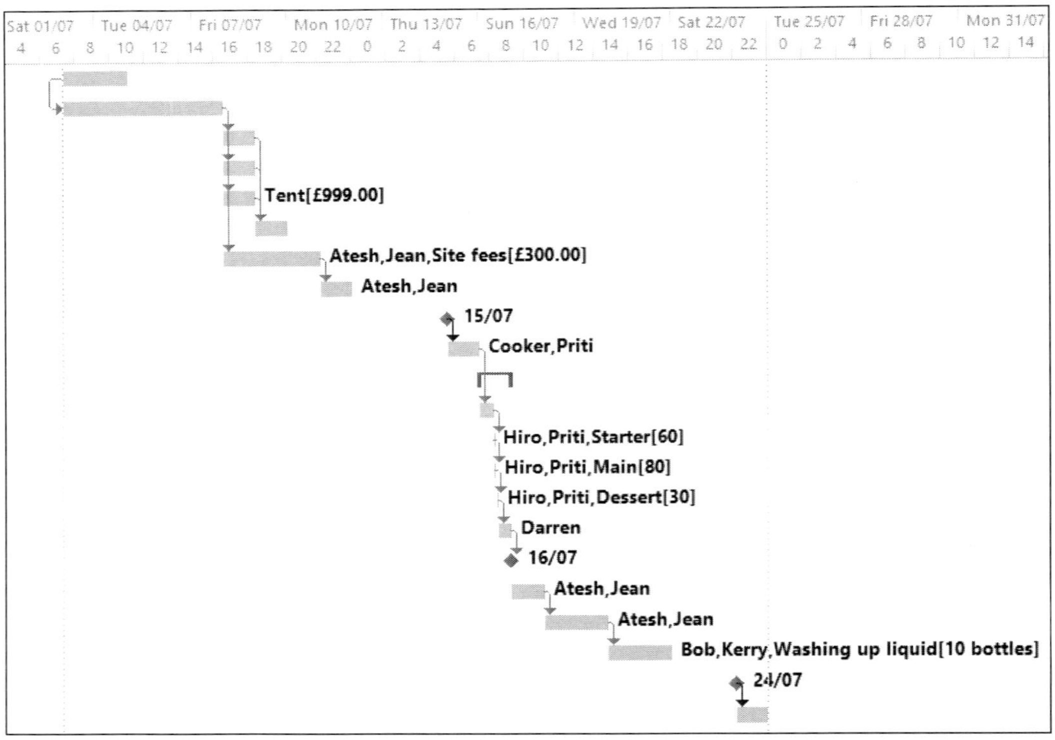

13. Save the project and leave it open for the next lesson.

*You are also able to add fixed costs to individual tasks, regardless of which resources are assigned to them. To do this, display the **VIEW** tab, click **Tables** and select **Cost**. Although useful for quickly drafting a simple project plan, it is always recommended that you create and assign cost resources instead. If you do decide to use the **Costs** table to add fixed costs, always remember to use the **Tables** button to return the view to **Entry** when you are finished.*

Driving Lesson 66 - Dealing with Change

Park and Read

Despite a project manager's best efforts and estimations, real life will rarely match a project plan exactly. Over time, the availability of workers may change, material costs may increase or decrease, and additional unexpected fees may be incurred.

Fortunately, it is very easy to add, change, delete and replace resources in *Project*.

Manoeuvres

1. With the **party** project still open from the previous lesson, display the **Resource Sheet**.

2. You have hired another cleaner for the garden party. In empty row **16**, add a new **Work** resource with the name **Ellen**. This new employee works for £10 per hour standard rate, £17 per hour overtime.

Ellen	Work		E		100%	£10.00/hr	£17.00/hr

3. By clicking and dragging on the **Row Heading Bar**, move row **16**, **Ellen**, up between rows **7** and **8**. *Ellen* should now appear directly below *Bob* on the **Resource Sheet**.

6	Kerry	Work		K	Cleaner
7	Bob	Work		B	Cleaner
8	Ellen	Work		E	

4. Add *Ellen* to the **Cleaner** group like *Kerry* and *Bob*.

5. Due to an error, resource **1**, **Atesh**, is being paid too little. Change his standard rate to £25 per hour.

A	Construction	100%	£25.00/hr	£0.00/hr	£0.00

6. Resources **4** and **5**, **Priti** and **Hiro**, both earn £15 per hour overtime. Correct the **Resource Sheet** to show this.

7. *Bob* has decided to leave the project and will no longer be available. Select row **7** on the **Row Heading Bar** and press <**Delete**> to remove this resource.

If you remove a resource, it will be automatically unassigned from any tasks.

8. Return to the **Gantt Chart** view. Notice that *Bob* is no longer assigned to task **20**.

Driving Lesson 66 - Continued

9. Using the **Assign Resources** dialog box, assign **Ellen** to task **20**.

10. Using the **Assign Resources** dialog box, change the **Tent** cost resource assigned to task **5**, **Hire tent**, to **£1500**.

	Resource Name	R/D	Units	Cost
✔	Tent			£1,500.00
	Atesh			

11. Update the number of washing up liquid bottles assigned to task **20**, **Clean up**, to **15 bottles**.

	Resource Name	R/D	Units	Cost
✔	Ellen		100%	£160.00
✔	Kerry		100%	£128.00
✔	Washing up liquid		15 bottles	£75.00

12. You have incorrectly assigned the waiter *Priti* to task **10**, **Cook food**. Select task **10**.

13. Using the **Assign Resources** dialog box, select **Priti** and click **Replace**. From the **Replace Resource** dialog box, select **Zak** instead.

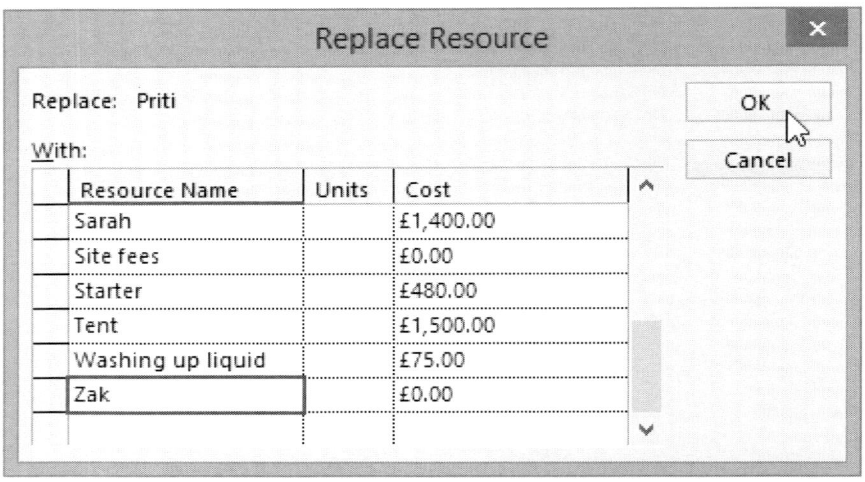

14. Click **OK** and the resource is replaced.

15. *Jean* has informed you that she will not be available to dismantle the party tent after the event. Select task **19**, **Take down tent**, and select **Jean** on the **Assign Resources** dialog box.

16. Click **Remove** to remove this resource from the task (the resource is not deleted, simply unassigned).

17. Close the **Assign Resources** dialog box.

18. Save the project and close it.

Driving Lesson 67 - Effort-Driven Scheduling

Park and Read

It is important to understand that there is a direct relationship between a task's duration and the resources assigned to complete it. For example, a ten day task will take one person 10 days to complete. That same task would also take two people 5 days, or five people 2 days.

*Work time is used to describe the amount of **effort** required to complete a task.*

Manoeuvres

1. Open the project **Effort**. This simple project has been created to illustrate the differences between duration and working time.

2. Display the **Resource Sheet** to find four work resources. Notice that each resource works for £10 per hour.

Resource Name	Type	Material Label	Initials	Group	Max. Units	Std. Rate
Peter	Work		P	Builder	100%	£10.00/hr
Fiona	Work		F	Builder	100%	£10.00/hr
Adya	Work		A	Builder	100%	£10.00/hr
Jaz	Work		J	Builder	100%	£10.00/hr

Project's default working time is 5 days per week (Mon-Fri), 8 hours per day.

3. Return to the **Gantt Chart** view and select task **1**, **Build north wall**. Notice that it currently takes 10 days to complete.

4. Open the **Assign Resources** dialog box. Select **Peter** from the list of resources and click **Assign**.

5. Notice that it currently costs **£800** to assign **Peter** to this task. This is calculated as 10 days x 8 hours x £10 (*Peter's* standard hourly rate).

	Resource Name	R/D	Units	Cost
✔	Peter		100%	£800.00
	Adya			
	Fiona			
	Jaz			

6. Next, select task **2**, **Build south wall** in the **Task List** (you do not need to close the **Assign Resources** dialog box to do this). Assign **Fiona**.

If you assign more than one work resource to a task, this will obviously increase the amount of "effort" (and therefore cost) required to complete it. However, you can also choose to reduce the duration of the task instead.

7. Assign **Adya** to this task also.

Driving Lesson 67 - Continued

8. Notice a scheduling icon, , has appeared to the left of this task's name in the **Task List**. Click this once and read the options available.

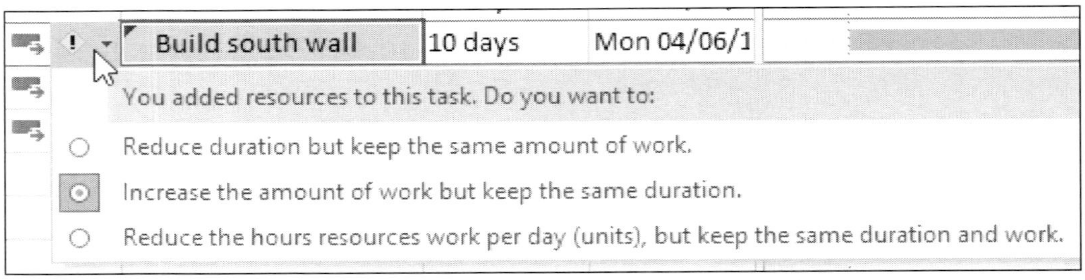

9. The default option is to **Increase the amount of work but keep the same duration.** This means the duration you set stays the same but, as two people are now working on the task, the amount of work doubles (and so do your costs).

10. Select **Reduce duration but keep the same amount of work.** The original amount of work now stays the same, but as two people are working on it, the duration is halved.

*A work resource only has a finite amount of working time available each day (8 hours by default). If you assign a resource to too many tasks at the same time, you will **overallocate** that resource (i.e. give it too many jobs to do).*

11. Select task **3**, **Build east wall**, and assign **Peter** to this task. Notice the overallocation icon, , that appears in the **Task List**. This is because *Peter* is already assigned to task **1**.

*To resolve a resource overallocation, you can simply delay tasks so that the overallocation does not occur. This is called **levelling**.*

12. On the **RESOURCE** tab, click **Level Resource**. Select **Peter** in the **Level Resources** dialog box and click **Level Now**. The third task is delayed so that *Peter* is no longer overallocated.

*Recall that a work resource can have a percentage of its **capacity** allocated to a task. However, if you do this, it will take longer to complete the task.*

13. Assign **Jaz** to task **4**, **Build west wall**. On the **Assign Resources** dialog box, change the **Units** to **50%**. The duration for task **4** is doubled as *Jaz* is only able to work on the task half of the time (i.e. 4 hours per day).

14. Click the scheduling icon, , that has appeared to the left of this task's name in the **Task List**. Select **Change the amount of work but keep the duration the same**.

15. The duration is reduced to 10 days again but, as *Jaz* is only working half of the time, the cost is halved to £400.

16. Save the project as **effort complete** and close it.

Driving Lesson 68 - Develop Your Skills

Park and Read

In this lesson you will add more detail to the **movie** project plan.

Manoeuvres

1. Open the project **movie** that you created earlier.

*An up-to-date model copy of the **movie** project is available in the data files folder **Training**. This is named **section9 movie**. If you would like to use this, open the project and save it as **movie** in the main data files folder.*

2. Display the **Resource Sheet** and enter the following resources (use default values unless otherwise specified):

	Resource Name	Type	Material Label	Std. Rate
1	Writer	Work		£50.00/hr
2	Reviewer	Work		£50.00/hr
3	Advisor	Work		£100.00/hr
4	Driver	Work		£10.00/hr
5	Set Builder	Work		£15.00/hr
6	Technicians	Work		£20.00/hr
7	Lead Actor	Work		£500.00/hr
8	Supporting Actor	Work		£500.00/hr
9	Extras Team	Work		£100.00/hr
10	Director	Work		£100.00/hr
11	Cameras	Work		£19/hr
12	Film	Material	reels	£50.00
13	Transport	Cost		
14	Tax	Cost		

3. Return to the **Gantt Chart** view.
4. Assign the resource **Writer** to tasks **5** and **7**.
5. Assign the resource **Reviewer** to tasks **6** and **8**.
6. Assign the resource **Advisor** to tasks **14** and **30**.
7. Assign the resources **Driver** and **Transport** to tasks **16** and **17**.
8. Assign the resource **Set Builder** to task **21**.
9. Assign the resource **Technicians** to task **23**.

Driving Lesson 68 - Continued

10. Assign the resources **Cameras** and **Film** to task **24**.

*To select and assign multiple resources on the **Assign Resources** dialog box, hold down <**Ctrl**> on your keyboard and click each resource.*

11. Assign the resources **Director**, **Extras Team**, **Lead Actor** and **Supporting Actor** to task **25**.

12. Finally, assign the resource **Tax** to task **30**.

13. You plan to take a stretched limousine to check out possible filming locations. A firm has quoted £1000 for a 10 days rental, and £1250 for a 15 day rental. Let's add these as fixed costs...

14. Select task **16** and, on the **Assign Resources** dialog box, enter a fixed **Transport** cost of **£1000**.

	Resource Name	R/D	Units	Cost
✔	Driver		100%	£800.00
✔	Transport			£1,000.00

15. Similarly, add a fixed **Transport** cost of **£1250** to task **17**.

16. The project's financial advisor has estimated that taxes incurred during filming will amount to £4000. Add a fixed **Tax** cost of **£4000** to task **30**.

17. *Keanu* and *Sandra*, the lead and supporting actor, have demanded a higher level of pay. Return to the **Resource Sheet** view and change the **Std. Rate** value for resources **7** and **8** to **£600/hr**.

18. The project's script reviewer shouldn't be paid as highly as the script writer. Reduce the **Std. Rate** value for resource **2** to **£30/hr**.

19. The **Driver** charges a fixed fee of £200 every time he is used (this is in addition to his £10 per hour standard rate). Enter **200** in the **Cost/Use** column for resource **4**.

Resource Name	Type	Material	Initials	Group	Max.	Std. Rate	Ovt.	Cost/Use
Writer	Work		W		100%	£50.00/hr	£0.00/hr	£0.00
Reviewer	Work		R		100%	£30.00/hr	£0.00/hr	£0.00
Advisor	Work		A		100%	£100.00/hr	£0.00/hr	£0.00
Driver	Work		D		100%	£10.00/hr	£0.00/hr	£200.00
Set Builder	Work		S		100%	£15.00/hr	£0.00/hr	£0.00
Technicians	Work		T		100%	£20.00/hr	£0.00/hr	£0.00
Lead Actor	Work		L		100%	£600.00/hr	£0.00/hr	£0.00
Supporting Actor	Work		S		100%	£600.00/hr	£0.00/hr	£0.00
Extras Team	Work		E		100%	£100.00/hr	£0.00/hr	£0.00
Director	Work		D		100%	£100.00/hr	£0.00/hr	£0.00
Cameras	Work		C		100%	£19.00/hr	£0.00/hr	£0.00
Film	Material	reels	F			£50.00		£0.00
Transport	Cost		T					
Tax	Cost		T					

20. Return to **Gantt Chart** view, save the project and close it.

Driving Lesson 69 - Revision

Park and Read

At the end of every section you get the chance to complete one or more revision exercises to develop your skills and prepare you for your ECDL certification test. You should aim to complete the following steps without referring back to the previous lessons.

Manoeuvres

1. Open the project **revision** that you created earlier.

*An up-to-date model copy of the **revision** project is available in the data files folder **Training**. This is named **section9 revision**. If you would like to use this, open the project and save it as **revision** in the main data files folder.*

2. Display the **Resource Sheet** and enter the following resources (use default values unless otherwise specified):

	Resource Name	Type	Material Label	Std. Rate
1	Advisor	Work		£50.00/hr
2	Building Team	Work		£500.00/d
3	Decorating Team	Work		£400.00/d
4	Fitting Team	Work		£600.00/d
5	Technicians	Work		£20.00/hr
6	Removals	Work		£20.00/hr
7	Packaging	Material	boxes	£3.00
8	Plaster	Material	boards	£20
9	Paint	Material	tins	£10
10	Bills	Cost		

*Note that resources **2**, **3** and **4** are paid by the day, not the hour.*

3. Return to the **Gantt Chart** view.
4. Assign the resource **Advisor** to tasks **7** and **11**.
5. Assign the resources **Building Team** and **Plaster** to task **13**. Increase the number of assigned **Plaster** units to **10 boards**.
6. Assign the resources **Decorating Team** and **Paint** to task **14**. Increase the number of assigned **Paint** units to **25 tins**.
7. Assign the resource **Fitting Team** to task **15**.

Driving Lesson 69 - Continued

8. Assign the resource **Packaging** to task **17**. Increase the number of assigned **Packaging** units to **50 boxes**.
9. Assign the resource **Technicians** to tasks **18**, **19**, **24**, **26** and **27**.
10. Assign the resource **Removals** to task **21**.
11. Finally, assign the cost resource **Bills** to task **28**. Enter the cost as **£129.50**.
12. A problem exists for tasks **18** and **19**. Can you tell what it is?
13. Use the **Level Resource** feature to correct the **Technicians** resource overallocation in tasks **18** and **19**.
14. Add the following new work resource to the **Resource Sheet**:

Resource Name	Type	Material Label	Std. Rate
Office Staff	Work		£13.00/hr

15. Packaging has increased in price to **£4.50** per box! Adjust the **Packaging** resource accordingly.
16. The project's **Building Team** are using less people and have reduced their daily rate to **£350** per day. Make this change.
17. You have decided that you do not need an advisor to help you. Delete resource **1**, **Advisor** (it will be automatically unassigned from any tasks).
18. Back on the **Gantt Chart**, assign the new resource, **Office Staff**, to task **25**, **Arrange office**.
19. Save the project and close any open files.

*A sample project named **section9 revision complete** can be found in the **Revisions** folder within the data files. You can use this to compare your work against a model solution.*

*Now complete the **Record of Achievement Matrix** at the back of the guide. You should only move on when confident with the topics and features described in this section.*

Section 10
Project Monitoring

By the end of this section you should be able to:

Review a project

Understand the critical path

View slack time

Display a baseline

Track a project

Track tasks

Update task progress

Reschedule incomplete work

Work through the **Driving Lessons** in this section to gain an understanding of the above features.

For each **Driving Lesson**, read all of the **Park and Read** instructions and then, if applicable, perform the numbered steps of the **Manoeuvres**. Complete the **Revision** exercise(s) at the end of the section to test your knowledge.

Driving Lesson 70 - Monitoring a Project

Park and Read

Once a project starts, it is important that you continually refer back to your plan to monitor tasks and check that they are on schedule. *Microsoft Project* makes this easy to do, with tools to track task progress, update schedules and reassign resources.

A project plan is not a static document. Refer to it frequently and keep it updated as the project progresses.

Unfortunately, very few projects go according to plan. Unexpected events occur which can often have a significant impact on the resources that you use, their cost, and the final delivery date of the project. For example, workers may leave, you may use more resources than you planned, or a task may simply take longer than you estimated.

If you update your project plan with progress information, you will often find that you are able to see resource and task-delay problems before they occur.

Risk management is a critical part of project planning. Constantly review your task durations and check that they are realistic and achievable. If you spot a potential problem area and time and budgets permit, you can assign more staff or resources, introduce lag time between tasks, or even reduce a resource's capacity so that it has a little free time each day to deal with problems.

In general, you can always avoid risk and speed up a project by adding more resources. However, this will usually cost more money to do. You will need to find a satisfactory balance between the two.

Unfortunately, there are also many other risk factors that you have little control over. These include resource supply issues, material failures, personnel problems, weather delays, natural disasters such as fire and flood, and changes in policies that govern how you employ people or use resources. The best advice for risks such as these is to consider and plan ahead where possible, build redundancy into your plan, and react immediately if they occur.

Building redundancy into a plan means adding extra resources that aren't immediately required. For example, you could purchase a little more work and material resources than you need. If a problem occurs, these resources can then be used to help.

Finally, to monitor and control a project effectively, regular meetings should be held to keep appropriate project members informed about task progress and issues that are anticipated. Afterwards, take action on the results of these meetings and revise the project plan accordingly.

Driving Lesson 71 - Critical Path

Park and Read

Once you have linked all of the tasks in a project, you can create a **critical path**. This is simply the name given to a single chain of **critical tasks** that, together, directly affect the start and finish date of the project.

Although most tasks are important, not all are critical. For example, a task that has no successor tasks is unlikely to be a critical task as its completion date probably does not affect the project's finish date.

All tasks in the critical path must finish on time if the project is to finish on time. Any delay along the critical path will result in the project finishing later than planned.

It is also true that any time saved on critical tasks will result in the project finishing earlier.

Manoeuvres

1. Open the project **Railway**.
2. Use the **Zoom Entire Project** button on the **VIEW** tab to view all of the **Gantt Chart** at once. This makes it easier to see the project's critical path.
3. Display the **GANTT CHART TOOLS - FORMAT** tab.
4. In the **Bar Styles** group, place a check in the **Critical Tasks** box.

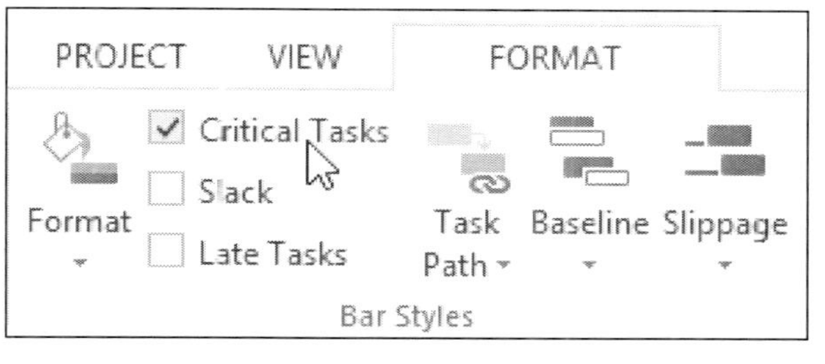

5. The project's critical path now appears. Examine the **Gantt Chart** and notice the chain of critical tasks that make up the project's critical path.

Critical tasks are displayed in red with non-critical tasks displayed in blue. The critical path is made up of the links between these tasks (also shown in red), linking the start of the project to the end.

6. At the moment, tasks **1**, **2**, **3**, **12**, **13** and **14** are all critical tasks. This is because they make up the critical path of tasks between the start and end date of the project.

Driving Lesson 71 - Continued

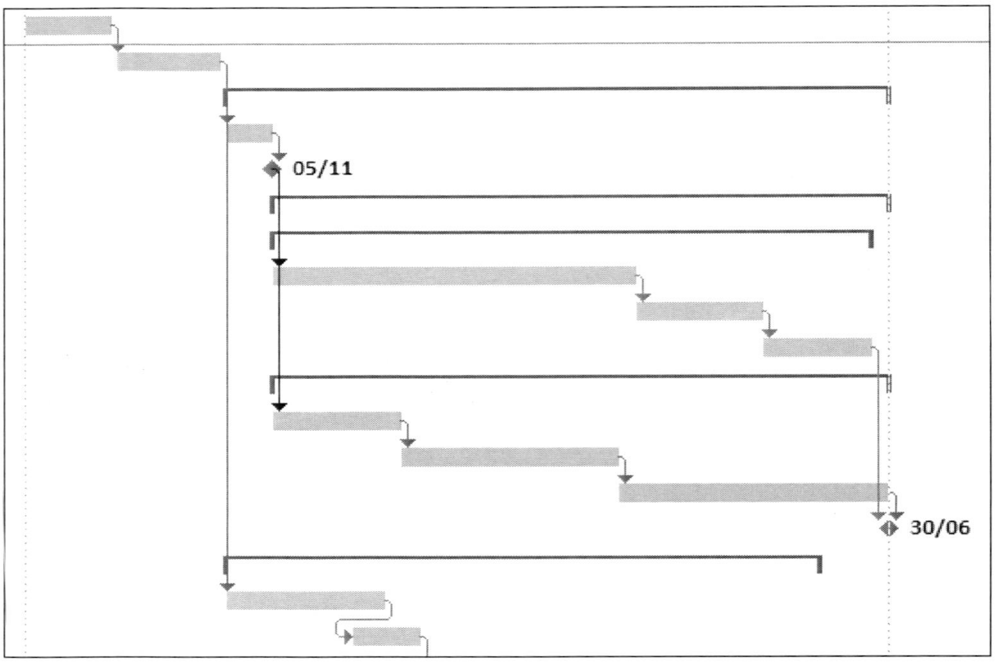

Any delay to the critical tasks shown will delay the whole project.

7. Notice that the **Duration** of task **13**, **York - Peterborough** is **60** days. Increase this to **70** days. As this is a critical task, the whole project is delayed by 10 days.

If non-critical task durations change and affect the end date of the project, these tasks will become critical and the critical path will move.

8. Change the **Duration** of task **9**, **Newcastle - Durham** to **70** days. The critical path moves.

*Some tasks have spare time available in which to "slip" should they overrun. This is known as **slack time** and can also be displayed on the **Gantt Chart**.*

9. In the **Bar Styles** group, place a check in the **Slack** box.
10. Notice the small black line that appears after some of the tasks. The **Duration** for those tasks can extend the length of that bar without affecting other tasks (or the end date of the project).

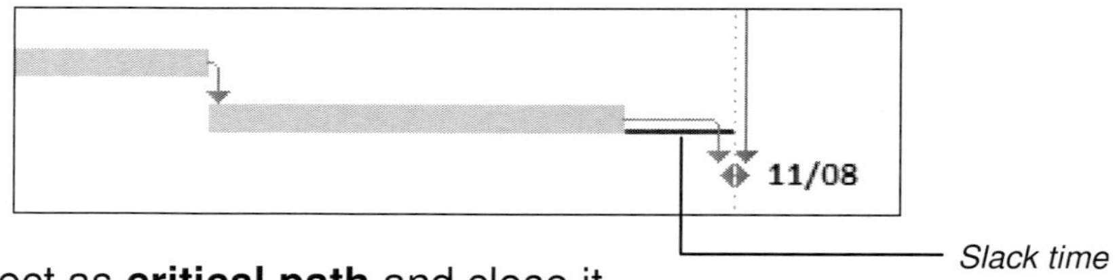

11. Save the project as **critical path** and close it.

Driving Lesson 72 - Creating a Baseline

Park and Read

Once you have completed your project plan you should create a **baseline**. This simply takes a "snapshot" of the project as it is right now so that you can refer back to it later.

Remember, a project plan is not a static document. During the project you will make changes to it, update progress, move and edit tasks, and reassign resources. A baseline allows you to look back at the project before these changes were made and compare the differences.

Accurately estimating task durations and correctly assigning resources is a skill that takes time to learn. To help, a baseline can be used at any time during the project to see where your initial project plan went wrong. The lessons you learn doing this will allow you to make better project plans next time.

Manoeuvres

1. Open the project **movie** that you created earlier.

*An up-to-date model copy of the **movie** project is available in the data files folder **Training**. This is named **section10 movie**. If you would like to use this, open the project and save it as **movie** in the main data files folder.*

2. To create a baseline for this project, display the **PROJECT** tab, click the **Set Baseline** button in the **Schedule** group and then select **Set Baseline** from the drop-down menu.
3. The **Set Baseline** dialog box appears. Make sure that both the **Set baseline** and **Entire project** options are selected.

*You can create more than one baseline in a project. To do this, simply select one of the other numbered baselines in the **Set baseline** drop-down box.*

4. Click **OK**. A snapshot of the project plan is now stored. Let's make a few changes to the project.
5. To raise finance for the movie, you have now arranged meetings with your solicitors and the bank. Task **11**, **Meet solicitors** will take only five days. Change the **Duration** of task **11** to **5d**.
6. Task **12**, **Meet banks**, will take a little longer than estimated. Change the duration of task **12** to **30d**.
7. Your advisor informs you that it will take longer than three days to hire all of the actors, engineers and technicians needed to complete the movie. Change the **Duration** for task **14**, **Employ people** to **10d**.

Driving Lesson 72 - Continued

8. Changes have now been made to the plan since you created the baseline. To compare these changes on the **Gantt Chart**, first display the **GANTT CHART TOOLS - FORMAT** tab.

9. Click the **Baseline** button in the **Bar Styles** group. Then, from the drop-down menu that appears, select the default **Baseline** entry (first in the list).

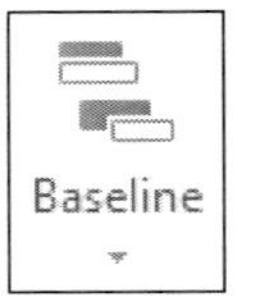

10. Examine the **Gantt Chart**. The tasks and durations saved in the baseline are now overlaid on top of the current tasks.

Baseline tasks and their durations are shown as half-height grey bars.

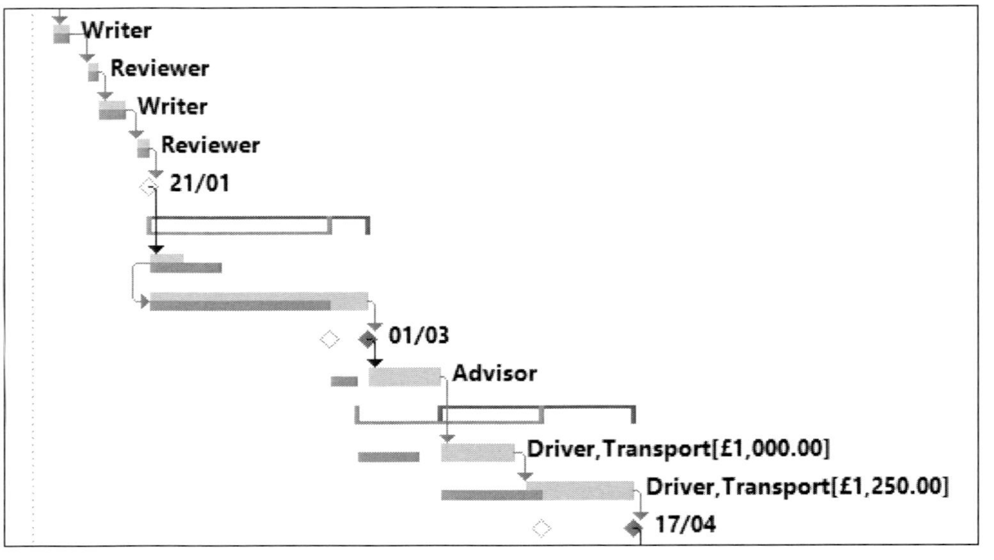

11. Notice the difference between the baseline and actual durations for tasks **11**, **12** and **14**. The knock-on effect of adjusting their durations can also be seen on all successor tasks.

It is at this point that the project manager can look at changing the plan to bring tasks back on track.

12. Increase the **Duration** of task **11** to **10d**. Then, decrease the **Duration** of task **12** to **25d** and task **14** to **3d**. This puts the plan back on track.

13. To hide the **Baseline**, click the **Baseline** button on the **GANTT CHART TOOLS - FORMAT** tab and select the saved **Baseline** again. The baseline is hidden but is still saved and can be viewed again later.

14. To delete the baseline completely, display the **PROJECT** tab, click **Set Baseline** and, from the options that appear, select **Clear Baseline.**

15. With the default **Clear baseline plan** and **Baseline** selected on the **Clear Baseline** dialog box, click **OK** and the baseline is deleted.

16. Save the project and leave it open for the next lesson.

Driving Lesson 73 - Updating Task Progress

Park and Read

A task's progress is measured as a percentage. It starts at **0% Complete** (not started) and increases until **100% Complete** (finished) is reached.

Manoeuvres

1. The **movie** project has been running for a few days now, so let's update task progress. Select task **2**, **Production meeting**.

*As updating task progress is such an important activity, there are specific buttons on the **Ribbon** to make it easy to do.*

2. This task is now finished, so click the **100% Complete** button, , in the **Schedule** group on the **TASK** tab. The task is marked as complete and a tick symbol appears in the **Indicators** column.

*Progress is a best-guess estimation – do not worry about trying to calculate an exact percentage (**0%**, **25%**, **50%**, **75%** and **100%** are usually adequate).*

3. Mark task **3**, **Find a writer** as **100% Complete** also.
4. Select tasks **5**, **6** and **7** together. Then click the **100% Complete** button to mark all of these tasks as complete together.
5. Another method of just updating a task's progress is to use the **Task Information** dialog box. Double click task **8**, **second review** in the **Task List** and increase the **Percent complete** to **100%**.

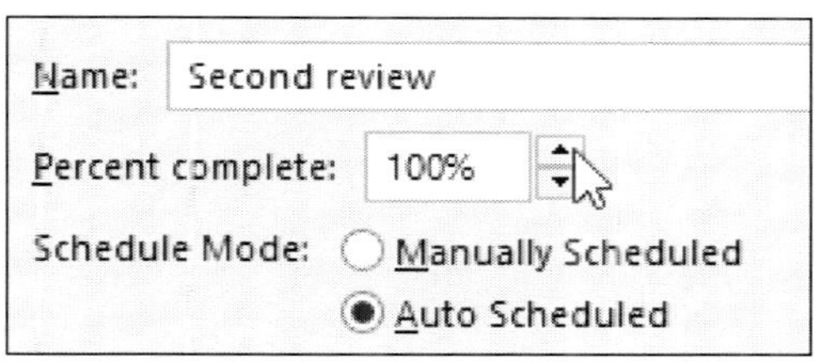

6. Click **OK**.
7. Update task **9**, **Complete script** to **100% Complete** also.

*Notice the **0%**, **25%**, **50%** and **75%** buttons in the **Schedule** group.*

8. You are currently meeting with solicitors and banks to raise finance. Update task **11** to **75% Complete** and task **12** to **25% Complete**.

*Percentage progress appears on the **Gantt Chart** as a darker line in the centre of the bar, .*

Driving Lesson 74 - Updating Project Progress

Park and Read

Rather than updating individual tasks one at a time, you can automatically update the progress of all tasks at once. Assuming everything has gone according to plan, you can do this to "bring the project up-to-date".

Manoeuvres

1. Time has passed and more of the **movie** project has been completed. You are currently working on task **16, Look locally**, so let's update the project plan...
2. Display the **PROJECT** tab and click **Update Project** in the **Status** group. The **Update Project** dialog box appears.
3. To demonstrate this feature, enter the date **03/03/2017** in the **Update work as complete through** box. This date falls during task **16**.
4. Leave **Set 0% - 100% complete** selected. This will update the progress of any completed task or task that is "in progress" (calculating the **Percentage complete** based on the duration elapsed).

If you select ***Set 0% or 100% complete only****,* Project *will set each finished task to 100% and all other tasks – including those in progress – to* ***0% Complete****.*

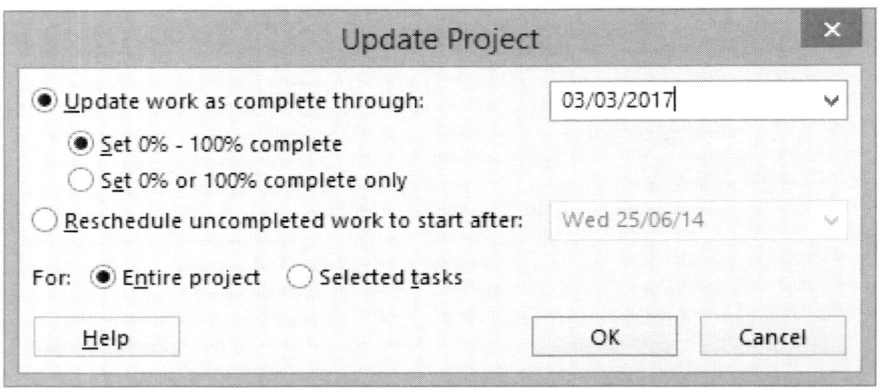

5. Click **OK**. A dialog box appears informing you that, due to constraints in the project, some tasks can't be automatically rescheduled.
6. As you aren't rescheduling uncompleted work – only updating progress – you can simply ignore this message and click **OK**.
7. Notice that all tasks up to *Friday, March 03, 2017* are automatically updated.
8. Save the project and leave it open for the next lesson.

Driving Lesson 75 - Rescheduling Work

Park and Read

If a delay occurs during a project that stops all work, you can automatically reschedule incomplete tasks to start again on another date. Tasks that were in progress will be split.

Manoeuvres

1. The **movie** project has been delayed by 7 days. Due to illness, you were unable to complete task **16**, **Look locally** as planned. Let's reschedule all incomplete tasks and resume the project.
2. Display the **PROJECT** tab and click **Update Project** in the **Status** group. The **Update Project** dialog box appears.
3. Select **Reschedule uncompleted work to start after**. Then, in the box to the right, enter **09/03/2017**.

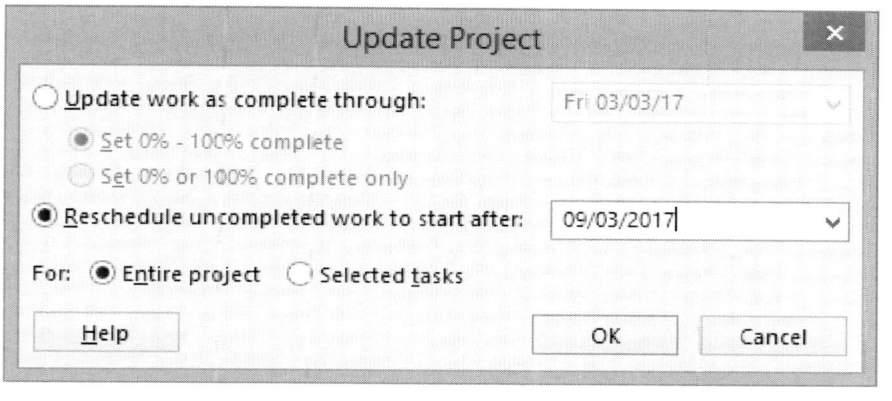

4. Click **OK**. A dialog box appears informing you that, due to constraints in the project, tasks can't be rescheduled.
5. Click **OK**. Task **16** is split and resumes on *Friday, March 10, 2017* (the day after **09/03/2017**). All successor tasks are also pushed back.

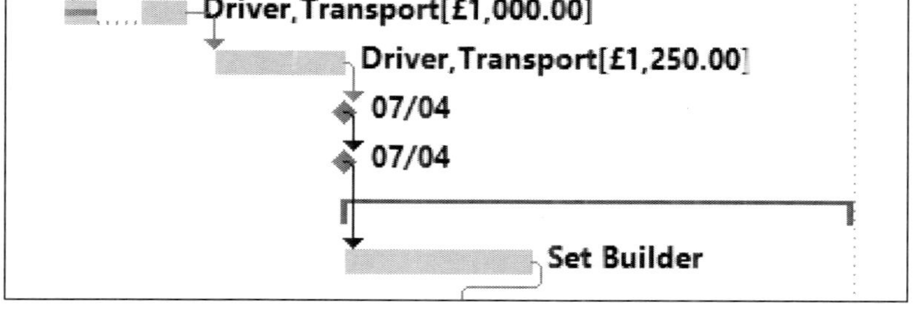

6. Despite the delay, you still need to meet the project's deadline in task **32**. Reduce the **Duration** for task **16** to **9d** to bring the project back on track.
7. Save the project and close it.

Driving Lesson 76 - Progress Lines

Park and Read

A **progress line** is simply a red line drawn down the **Gantt Chart** which shows, for any given date, the tasks that are on schedule or running late.

Manoeuvres

1. Open the project **Fun Run**. This simple project was created to help organise a fun run for a local charity.
2. Notice that progress has already been entered for a number of tasks. Let's display a progress line to see how well the project is going...
3. Display the **PROJECT** tab and click the **Status Date** button in the **Status** group (it currently reads **17/06/18**).
4. Enter **08/06/2018** – a date in the middle of the project – and click **OK**.

*The **Status Date** is simply a date in the project that you want to focus on. It usually matches the date that you entered when updating task progress.*

5. Display the **GANTT CHART TOOLS - FORMAT** tab and click the **Gridlines** button. From the options that appear, select **Progress Lines**.
6. The **Progress Lines** dialog box appears. Select the **Display** checkbox under **Current progress line** and make sure **At project status date** is selected.
7. Click **OK** and a progress line appears on the **Gantt Chart**. A circle, ⌖, appears on any task that is currently in progress on the **Status Date**.

*You can also set a progress line to appear on another date by simply changing the **Status Date** in the **Status** group.*

8. Red circles on the progress line indicates active tasks that are on schedule. However, notice the "spikes" pointing left.

If the progress line shows spikes to the left, ⌖<, this highlights an active task that has not been completed as scheduled.

9. Task **6** should have completed by the **Status Date** but is only 75% complete at the moment. A left spike on the progress line indicates it is running late. Mark task **6** as **100% complete** and the spike is removed.
10. To hide the progress line, open the **Progress Lines** dialog box again and remove the tick from the **Display** checkbox. Click **OK**.
11. Close the project without saving.

Driving Lesson 77 - Revision

Park and Read

At the end of every section you get the chance to complete one or more revision exercises to develop your skills and prepare you for your ECDL certification test. You should aim to complete the following steps without referring back to the previous lessons.

Manoeuvres

1. Open the project **revision** that you created earlier.

*An up-to-date model copy of the **revision** project is available in the data files folder **Training**. This is named **section10 revision**. If you would like to use this, open the project and save it as **revision** in the main data files folder.*

2. Set a **Baseline** for the entire project.
3. Display the **Critical Path**.
4. Mark tasks **1** to **11** as **100% Complete**.
5. Set task **13**, **Builders** to **50% complete**.
6. Increase the **Duration** of task **15**, **Fitters** to **2w**.
7. Display the **Baseline**. Notice the differences – the project now misses its deadline in task **30**.
8. Get the project back on schedule by reducing the duration of task **15**, **Fitters** to **1w** again.
9. Hide the **Baseline** but do not delete it.
10. All tasks up to *Monday, October 16, 2017* are now complete (**16/10/2017**). Update project progress to show this.
11. Save the project and close any open files.

*A sample project named **section10 revision complete** can be found in the **Revisions** folder within the data files. You can use this to compare your work against a model solution.*

*Now complete the **Record of Achievement Matrix** at the back of the guide. You should only move on when confident with the topics and features described in this section.*

Section 11
Project Views

By the end of this section you should be able to:

Scroll to tasks

Show and hide Task List columns

Sort and filter tasks

View network diagrams

Work through the **Driving Lessons** in this section to gain an understanding of the above features.

For each **Driving Lesson**, read all of the **Park and Read** instructions and then, if applicable, perform the numbered steps of the **Manoeuvres**. Complete the **Revision** exercise(s) at the end of the section to test your knowledge.

Driving Lesson 78 - Gantt Chart Navigation

Park and Read

As you now know, the display of tasks over time is displayed on a **Gantt Chart** to the right of the **Task List**. There are lots of useful tips to help you move around this chart quickly and easily.

Manoeuvres

1. Open the file **Railway** and examine the **Gantt Chart**. The scrollbars at the bottom and right can be used to move the view horizontally and vertically.
2. Press <**Alt →**> to scroll the view to the right a little. Press <**Alt ←**> to scroll the timescale to the left again.
3. Press <**Page Down**> to move the view down one screen. Press <**Page Up**> to move up again.
4. Press <**Alt End**> to view the end of the project on the **Gantt Chart**. Press <**Alt Home**> to view the start of the project.

*The **Scroll to Task** feature enables you to select a task in the **Task List** and move to its bar in the **Gantt Chart**.*

5. Select task **31**, **Open New Line** in the **Task List**. Then click the **Scroll to Task** button in the **Editing** group on the **TASK** tab. The **Gantt Chart** view jumps to this task's bar.

*The **Go To** dialog box can be used to move to and select a task in the **Task List**. This is useful in complex projects which may contain a lot of tasks.*

6. Press <**F5**> to open the **Go To** dialog box.

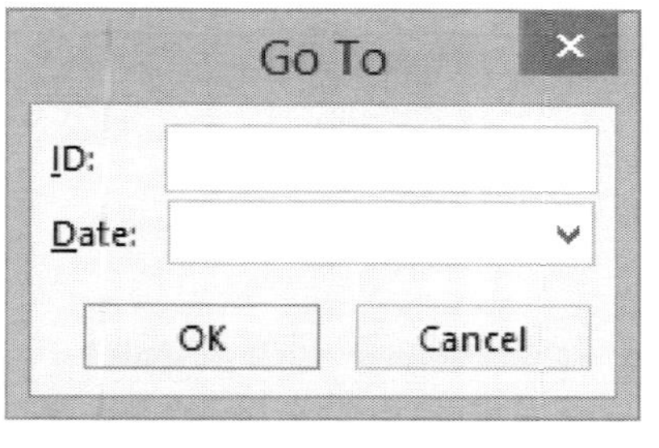

7. Enter **18** into the **ID** box and click **OK**. Task **18** is selected. Notice that the task bar is scrolled into view in the **Gantt Chart**.
8. Press <**F5**> and enter **1** into the **ID** box and click **OK** to return to the start of the project.
9. Close the project <u>without</u> saving.

Driving Lesson 79 - Task List Columns

Park and Read

A lot of the information that you enter using the **Task Information** and **Assign Resources** dialog boxes can be input directly into the **Task List**.

Manoeuvres

1. Open the project **movie** that you created earlier.

*An up-to-date model copy of the **movie** project is available in the data files folder **Training**. This is named **section11 movie**. If you would like to use this, open the project and save it as **movie** in the main data files folder.*

2. Place your mouse pointer over the dividing bar between the **Task List** and **Gantt Chart**.

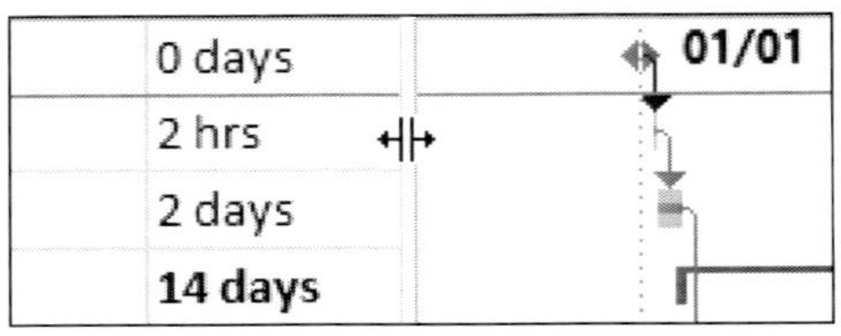

3. The mouse pointer changes to, ⇹. Click and drag the dividing bar to the far right of the screen to increase the space occupied by the **Task List**.
4. Examine the various columns in the **Task List**. Notice the **Start**, **Finish**, **Predecessors** and **Resource Names** columns. You can directly enter values here to create and change task start and end dates, resources and links to predecessor tasks.
5. Notice that the final column is labelled **Add New Column**. Let's use this to add new columns to the **Task List**.

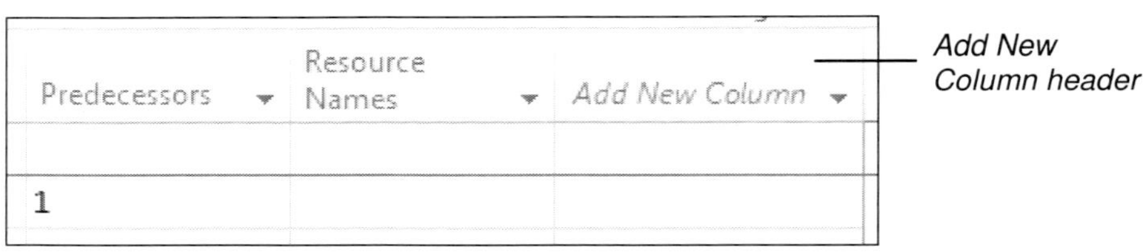

6. Click the **Add New Column** header and examine the comprehensive list of columns available. Select **% Complete** to show this column and the values entered for each task.

*You can scroll the **Task List** horizontally if you need to.*

7. Click **Add New Column** and select **Deadline** to display this column. Only task **32**, **Movie complete** has a value entered here. The rest are set as **NA** for *Not Applicable*.

Driving Lesson 79 - Continued

8. Add the **Fixed Cost** column.

Recall that you are able to add fixed costs to individual tasks, regardless of which resources are assigned to them. However, although these are useful for quickly drafting a simple project plan, it is always recommended that you create and assign cost resources instead.

9. Add the **Constraint Date** column.

10. Add the **Milestone** column.

11. Finally, add the **Cost** column.

12. You have now completed task **16**, **Look locally**. Click once in the **% Complete** cell for task **16** to select it. Then type **100%** and press <**Enter**>.

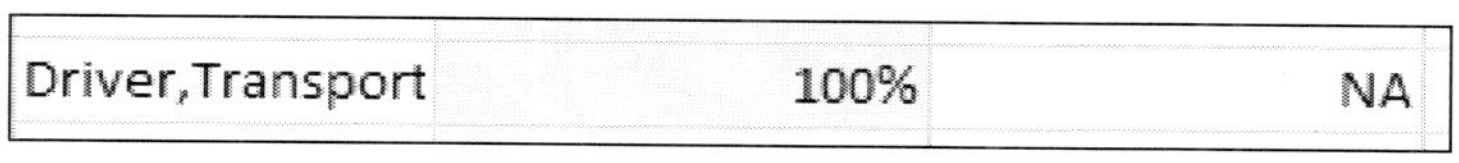

13. Similarly, set the **% Complete** for tasks **17** and **18** to **100%**.

*Notice that summary task **15** is **100%** complete when all subtasks are **100%**.*

14. Click once in the **Resource Names** cell for task **11**, **Meet solicitors**. Then, click the drop-down arrow and select **Advisor** from the list of resources that appears.

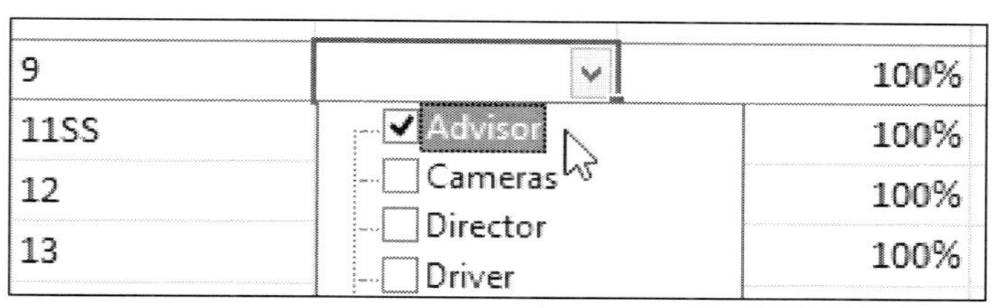

15. Press <**Enter**> to confirm the change. The resource is assigned.

*You can use the techniques described in this lesson to change any task properties shown in the **Task List**. However, as a beginner, you may find it easier to use the dedicated **Task Information** dialog box instead.*

16. It is easy to hide any column in the **Task List**. For example, right-click the **Constraint Date** column header. From the shortcut menu that appears, select **Hide Column**. The column is hidden.

17. Hide the **Fixed Cost** and **Milestone** columns too.

18. Leave the project open for the next lesson.

Driving Lesson 80 - Sorting and Filtering Tasks

Park and Read

Tasks in the **Task List** can be sorted by date, priority, and cost. They can also be filtered to display only critical tasks or milestones.

Manoeuvres

1. Using the **movie** project, you would like to see which tasks will take the longest time to complete. Click the drop-down arrow on the header of the **Duration** column.

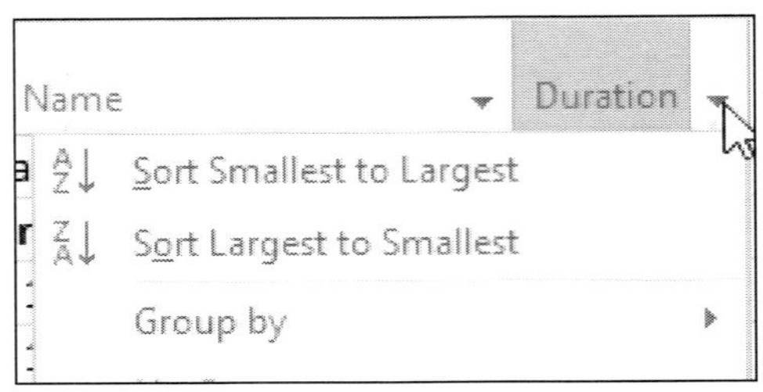

2. Select **Sort Largest to Smallest**. The summary task **Shoot movie** will take the longest time in total.
3. Which task starts the earliest? Sort the **Start Date** column *earliest to latest* to find out.
4. Which task costs the most to complete? Try sorting the **Cost** column *largest to smallest* to find out.
5. Try experimenting with different sorts.

*Filtering allows you to customise the **Task List** and only show tasks that match specific criteria (e.g. tasks that have not started yet or are milestones).*

6. To filter and view only the tasks that have not been started yet, click the drop-down arrow on the **% Complete** column. This time, click **Filters** and, from the submenu that appears, select **Not Started**.
7. Only tasks that have not been started yet now appear in the **Task List**.

Notice how a filter icon, 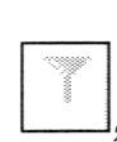*, appears at the top of the column.*

8. Click on the filter icon and select **Clear Filter from % Complete**. All tasks are shown again.

*The **Filter** feature in the **Data** group can be used to perform quick filters.*

9. On the **VIEW** tab, click the **Filter** drop-down list, 

, in the **Data** group. Select **Critical** to show only critical tasks.

Driving Lesson 80 - Continued

10. Next, filter the tasks to show only **Milestones**.

11. To remove whichever filter is active, click the **Filter** drop-down button again and select **[No Filter]**.

12. Experiment and try some of the other filters available.

*If you change the view of the **Gantt Chart**, you can quickly restore it to its default setting at any time. This resets the view window and removes any sorts and filters that are active.*

13. To quickly restore the **Gantt Chart** which may now be hidden, display the **VIEW** tab and click the drop-down arrow on the **Gantt Chart** button in the **Task Views** group.

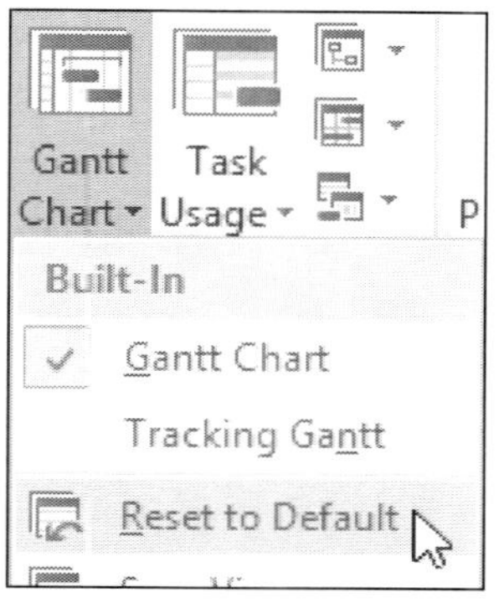

14. From the menu that appears, select **Reset to Default** and click **Yes**. The **Gantt Chart** view is reset and any sorts or filters that were active are removed.

15. Use the **Zoom Entire Project** button to view all of the **Gantt Chart** again.

*To return to the start of a project, recall that you can also press <**F5**> to **Go To** a task directly. Enter **1** in the **ID** box and click **OK**.*

16. Save the project and close it.

Driving Lesson 81 - Network Diagrams

Park and Read

A **Network Diagram** is a simple, graphical view of a project. It emphasises the relationships between tasks rather than their schedule and duration.

Network diagrams look like flowcharts and are ideal for creating a simple overview of a project for others.

Manoeuvres

1. Open the project **Farm**. This simple project is currently displayed as a **Gantt Chart**.
2. On the **VIEW** tab, click the **Network Diagram** button in the **Task Views** group (click the button's icon, not its drop-down menu).
3. The project's **Network Diagram** view appears. Notice that tasks now appear in coloured boxes connected by arrows.

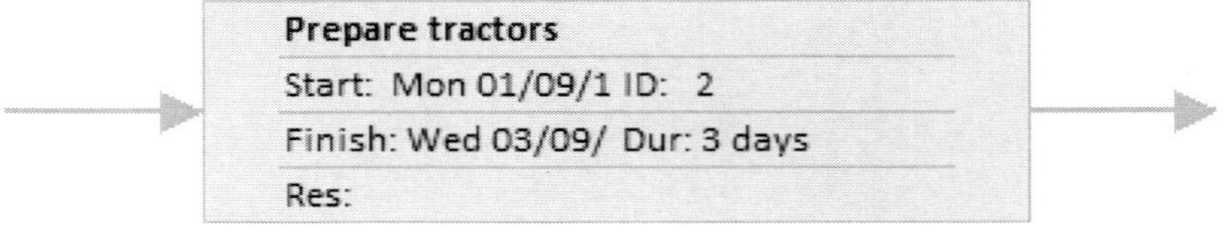

Task boxes show a task's name, duration, start/finish dates and assigned resources (if any).

4. Use the window's scrollbars to move around the diagram and see more of it. Notice how tasks appear in the diagram in the order they are scheduled to start, one after the other.

The arrows connecting tasks again show predecessors and successors. Pink boxes are critical tasks; blue boxes are non-critical tasks.

5. Display the **NETWORK DIAGRAM TOOLS - FORMAT** tab and select the **Link Labels** option. The link types now appear between boxes.

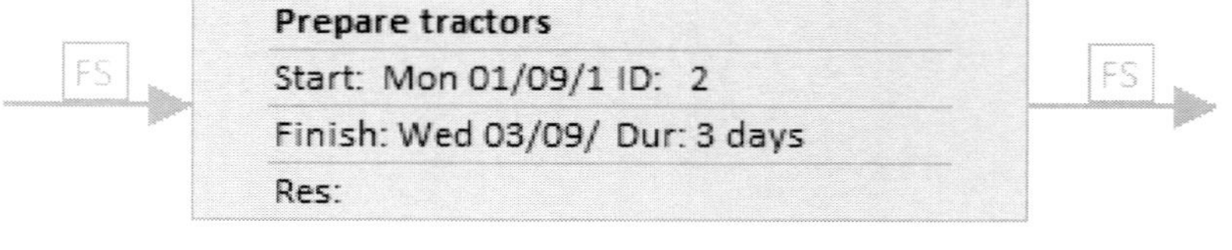

6. Use the **Zoom** controls to zoom out and see the entire diagram at once.
7. To see the detail on a task, place the mouse pointer over it and it is magnified. Try this with any task in the diagram.
8. On the **NETWORK DIAGRAM TOOLS - FORMAT** tab, click the **Box Styles** button in the **Format** group.

Driving Lesson 81 - Continued

9. The **Box Styles** dialog box shows a list of the possible task types and the style of box used to represent them. Click on each item below **Style setting for** and observe the **Preview** that appears.

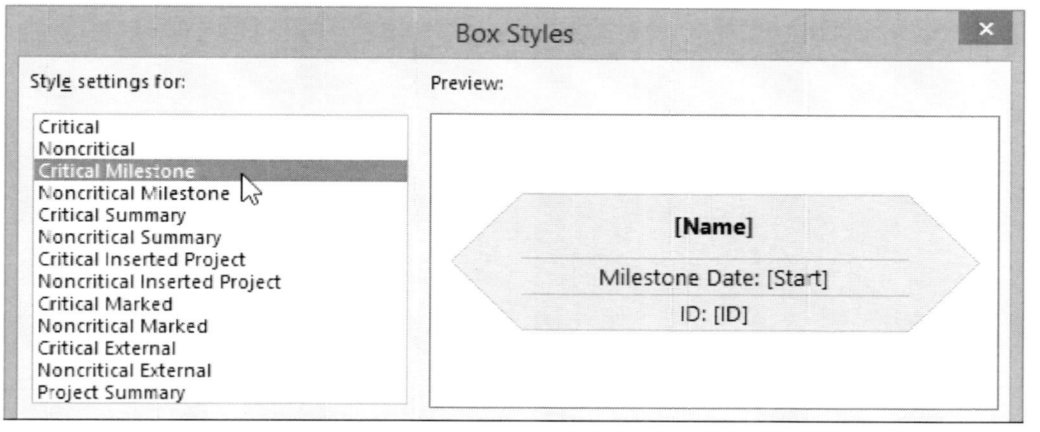

10. Click **Cancel** to close the **Box Styles** dialog box.

11. Select task **2**, **Prepare Tractors** in the **Network Diagram** by clicking it once. Then, display the **TASK** tab and click **100% Complete** in the **Schedule** group

12. The task is marked as complete. It will now appear with a large cross to indicate it is finished.

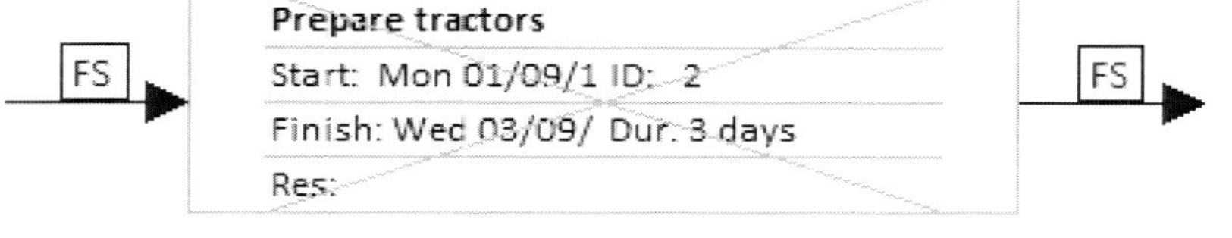

*You can select another task to view the changes made to task **2**. You can also zoom in to view each task in more detail.*

13. Select task **3**, **Prepare barn for storage**. Mark this task as **50% Complete** and notice the effect. It appears with a single line through it.

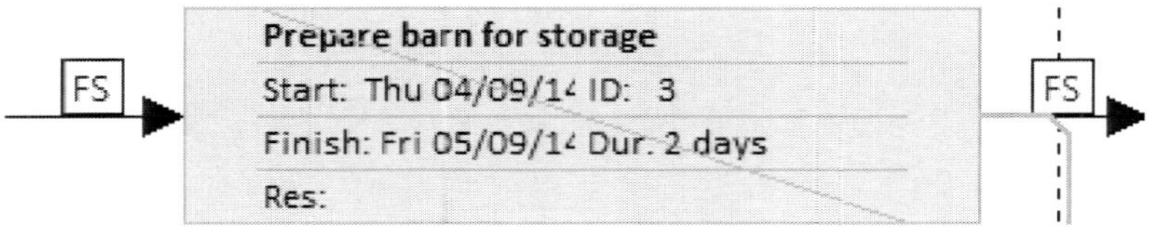

14. Save the project as **network diagram**.

15. Finally, try some of the other views in the **Task Views** group. In particular, try **Task Usage** view and **Calendar** view. Consider how each provides a different view of the same project.

16. When you are finished, close the **network diagram** project without saving any changes.

Driving Lesson 82 - Revision

Park and Read

At the end of every section you get the chance to complete one or more revision exercises to develop your skills and prepare you for your ECDL certification test. You should aim to complete the following steps without referring back to the previous lessons.

Manoeuvres

1. Open the project **revision** that you created earlier.

*An up-to-date model copy of the **revision** project is available in the data files folder **Training**. This is named **section11 revision**. If you would like to use this, open the project and save it as **revision** in the main data files folder.*

2. Add the **% Complete** and **Cost** columns to the **Task List**.
3. Hide the **Predecessors** and **Resource Names** columns.
4. Use the **% Complete** column in the **Task List** to mark task **19** as **100%** complete.
5. Similarly, use the **% Complete** column to mark task **20** as **50%** complete.
6. Sort tasks in the **Task List** by order of **Cost** (**Largest to Smallest**). Summary task **12** should cost the most to complete.
7. Sort the **Task List** by **Start Date** instead (**Earliest to Latest**).
8. Apply a filter so that only incomplete tasks are shown.
9. View the project's network diagram.
10. Return to the project's **Gantt Chart**.
11. Remove the filter and redisplay all **30** tasks.
12. Save the project and close any open files.

*A sample project named **section11 revision complete** can be found in the **Revisions** folder within the data files. You can use this to compare your work against a model solution.*

*Now complete the **Record of Achievement Matrix** at the back of the guide. You should only move on when confident with the topics and features described in this section.*

Section 12 Printing

By the end of this section you should be able to:

Use print preview

Change print settings

Adjust page setup

Add headers and footers

Print Task List columns and notes

Work through the **Driving Lessons** in this section to gain an understanding of the above features.

For each **Driving Lesson**, read all of the **Park and Read** instructions and then, if applicable, perform the numbered steps of the **Manoeuvres**. Complete the **Revision** exercise(s) at the end of the section to test your knowledge.

Driving Lesson 83 - Print Preview

Park and Read

All project views such as **Gantt Charts** and **Network Diagrams** can be printed. Before you do this, however, it is best to preview them first.

Print previewing also lets you see how a project will appear when saved as a PDF document.

Manoeuvres

1. Open the project **Railway**.
2. Although any project view can be printed, the default **Gantt Chart** is the most popular. Display the **FILE** tab and select **Print**.
3. The **Print** screen appears showing a preview of page **1 of 6** of the **Gantt Chart** as it will be printed.

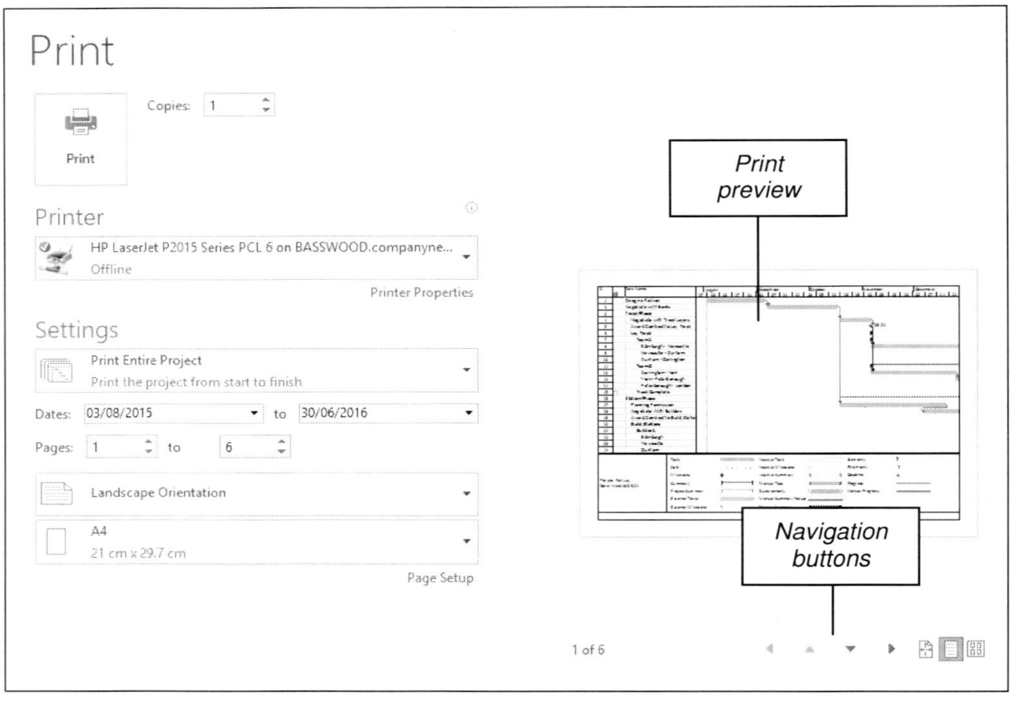

Other pages in the print can be viewed by clicking the navigation buttons found under the preview. If any of the buttons are ghosted (inactive) it means that there are no more pages to view in that direction.

4. Move the mouse pointer over the print preview. It changes to a magnifying glass, . Click anywhere on the print preview to zoom into that area. Click a second time to zoom out again.
5. View all of the pages in the print using the navigation buttons.

Driving Lesson 84 - Print Settings

Park and Read

The **Print** screen is used to select a **Printer** to send your project to. It can also be used to directly adjust a number of popular print settings such as page orientation and page size.

Manoeuvres

1. Examine the options on the left of the **Print** screen. Notice that you can adjust the number of **Copies** to print and select a **Printer** from those available to you.

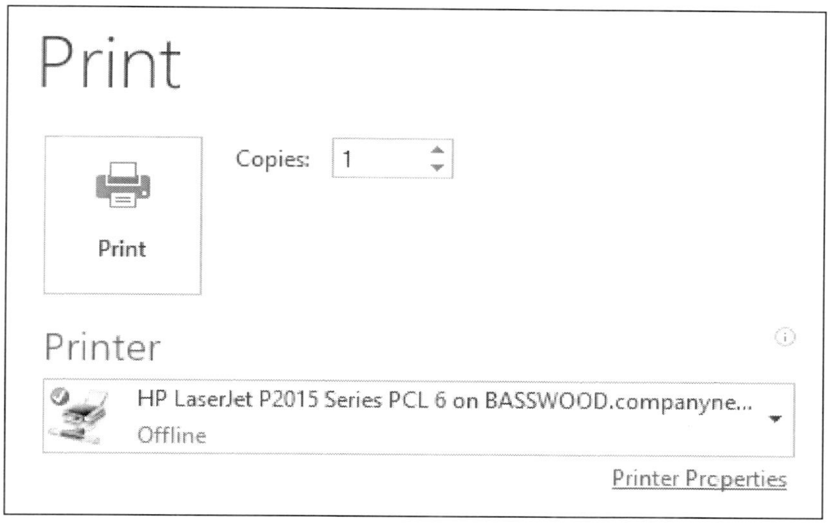

*The **Printer Properties** link can be used to adjust settings specific to the selected printer (e.g. colour options, print quality and print speed).*

2. Examine the **Settings** section and then click the **Print Entire Project** button. The options that appear allow you to print all or parts of a project.

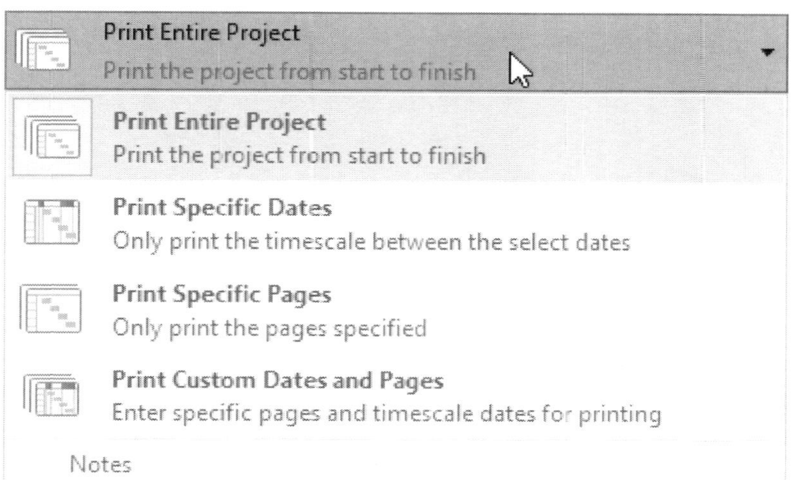

Driving Lesson 84 - Continued

*Selecting **Print Specific Dates** allows you to specify a start and end date. Only tasks that fall within these two dates will then be printed. This is sometimes useful when you only want to print a small part of a project.*

*Selecting **Print Specific Pages** simply allows you to print certain pages.*

3. The default option to print the entire project is ideal. Click **Print Entire Project** to keep this setting.

*The **Settings** section also allows you to change page orientation and paper size.*

4. Click the **Landscape Orientation** button.

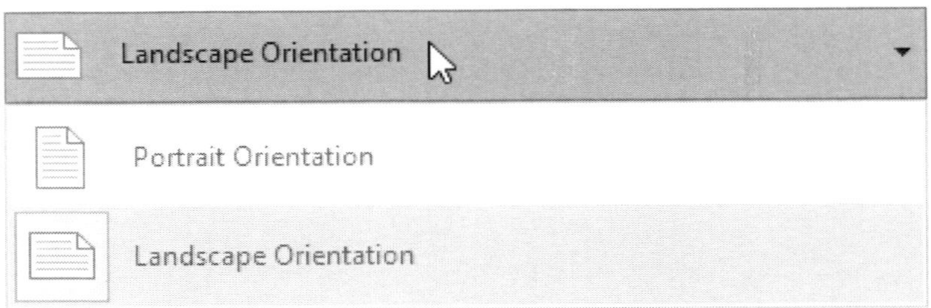

5. **Landscape** is the default page orientation. Click **Portrait Orientation** to see the difference in the print preview.
6. Landscape orientation is nearly always better for printing project plans. Click the button now labelled **Portrait Orientation** and select **Landscape Orientation** again.
7. Click the **A4** paper size button. Scroll down the list to view the available paper sizes available.
8. Select **A3** to see the effect. Printing on bigger paper sizes allows you to see more of a project plan at one time.
9. Standard **A4** is usually best, so click the button now labelled **A3** and select **A4** again.

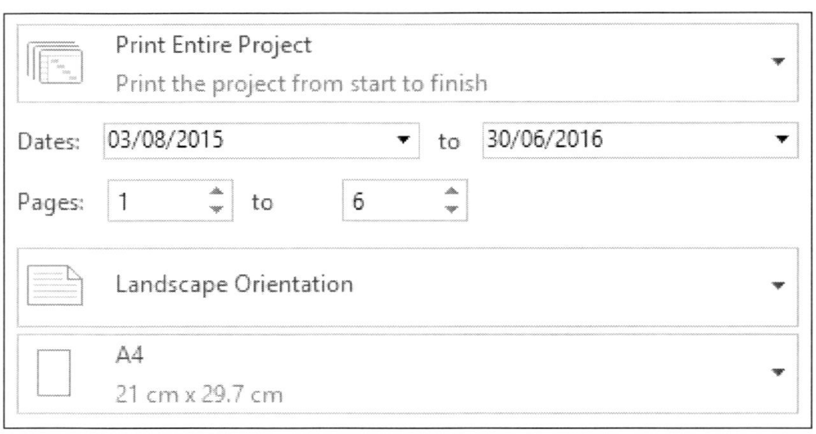

Driving Lesson 85 - Advanced Page Setup

Park and Read

The **Page Setup** dialog box gives you access to a range of more complex print features, such as page margins, page scaling and headers and footers.

Manoeuvres

1. Locate the **Page Setup** link at the bottom right of the **Settings** section.

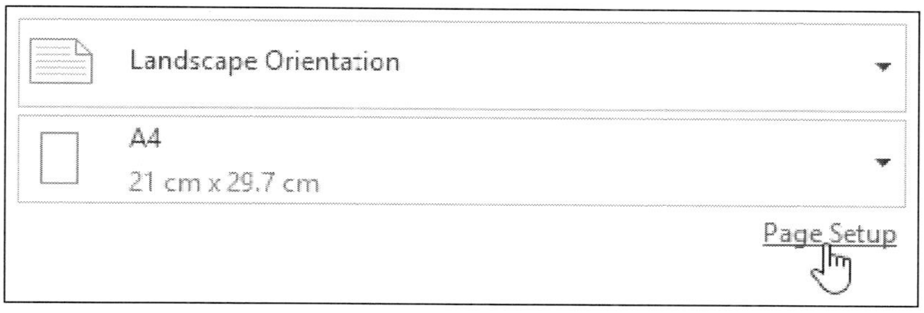

2. Click this once to display the **Page Setup** dialog box.
3. On the **Page** tab, examine the **Scaling** options below the **Orientation** settings. Scaling can be used to shrink or stretch the view of a project plan so it can fit on a specific number of pages.
4. Select **Fit to** and leave the default options as **1 pages wide by 1 tall**. This will shrink the plan so that it fits on a single page.

5. Click **OK** to return to the print preview and see the effect.
6. Click **Page Setup** again. This time, display the **Margins** tab. The options available here allow you to adjust the space between the edge of the page and the project plan (most printers require a small margin).
7. The margins are all **1.27** cm by default, which is ideal for most uses. To demonstrate the effect of changing them, however, change all to **3** cm.

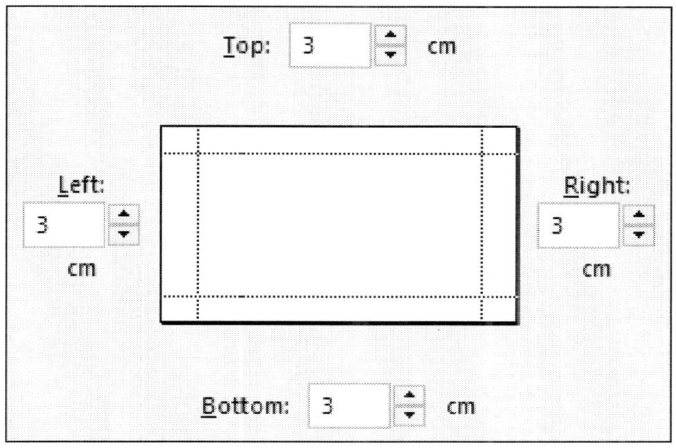

Driving Lesson 85 - Continued

8. Click **OK** to return to the print preview and see the effect. The space between the edge of the page and the project plan increases.

9. Click **Page Setup** again and change the **Top**, **Bottom**, **Left** and **Right** margins back to the default **1.27** cm.

10. Next, display the **Header** tab on the **Page Setup** dialog box. The options available here allow you to add text to the *top* of every printed page.

11. The **Center** tab is currently selected below the **Preview**. In the text box, enter **My Project Plan**.

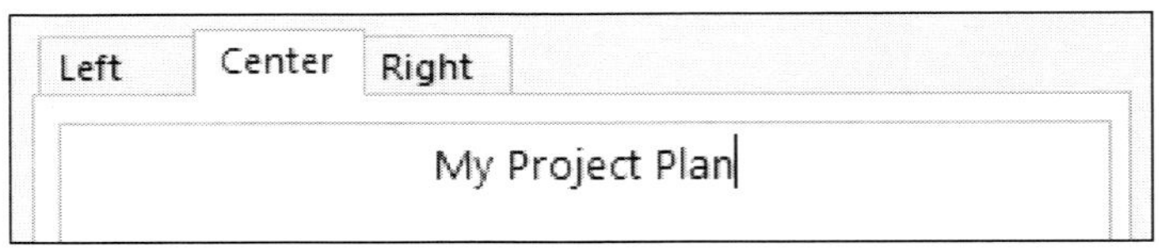

12. Click the **Footer** tab. The options available here allow you to add text to the bottom of every printed page.

*You can insert a variety of useful **field codes** in a header or footer. These are automatically updating values like **Page Number**, **Project Title**, **Company Name**, etc. Where relevant, this information is taken from the **Properties** dialog box set up at the start of the project*

13. The **Center** tab is currently selected below the **Preview**. Drop-down the **General** box, select **Project Title** and then click the **Add** button. The project title is placed in the centre of the header as a field code.

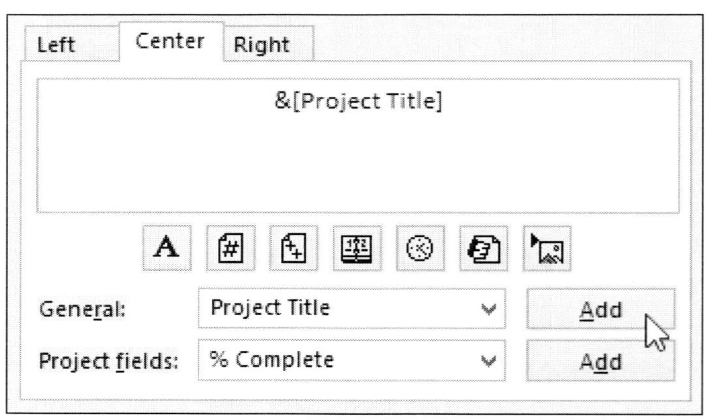

*The field code **&[Project Title]** will be replaced with the relevant project title text when printed. An example is provided in the **Preview** box.*

14. Display the **Left** tab and insert the **Page Number** field. Then, insert the **Company Name** field on the right tab.

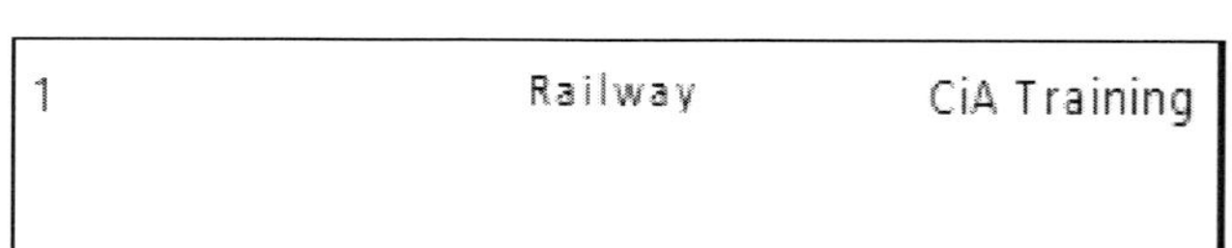

Driving Lesson 85 - Continued

15. Next, click the **Legend** tab. The **Legend** is a useful area on the printed page that briefly describes the different types of **Gantt Chart** bar (e.g. task bars, summary task bars, milestones, progress, deadlines, etc).

*Notice the **Legend on:** settings. These can be used to turn the legend off completely or include it on its own page.*

16. Click the **View** tab. This contains options to control what is printed.

By default, Project *only prints the first two columns in the **Task List**. You can change this using the **Print first** option.*

17. Check **Print first** and change the **columns on all pages** to **6**. The first six columns of the **Task List** will now appear to the left of the **Gantt chart**.

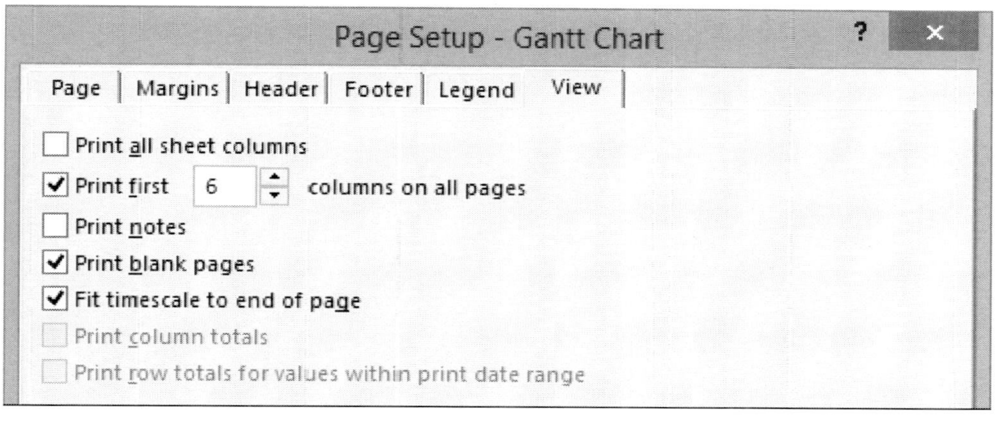

18. Click **OK** to see the effect the changes have had to the appearance of the preview.
19. Click the **Page Setup** link again and display the **View** tab (if not already displayed). The **Task Name** and **Duration** columns will be sufficient: change the **Print first** box to **4**.
20. Remove the check from **Print blank pages**.
21. Check **Print notes**; this will print any notes added to the project on their own page.
22. Click **OK** to see the effect the changes have had to the appearance of the preview.

Driving Lesson 86 - Printing

Park and Read

Projects are often printed and placed in a communal area where key personnel can see it. This allows everyone to see upcoming work, responsibilities and task progress.

You will usually print a project plan across multiple pages. These pages are designed to be placed side-by-side so that the whole project plan can be seen.

Manoeuvres

1. You can increase the number of copies of a print by replacing the default **1** in the **Copies** box with another number of your choice. For now, leave **Copies** as **1**.

2. Notice that your default printer is currently selected under **Printer**. Click the **Printer** drop-down button to display a list of available printers; all printers installed on your computer are visible here.

3. Click to select the printer you would like to print to.

In work and education you may have access to many printers. Try to find the name of the one closest to you. In some situations you may also be charged for paper and printing, so be careful what you print.

4. Click the large **Print** button to print a copy of the project on your chosen printer. You will automatically return to the previous **Gantt Chart** view.

*Alternatively, click the **Back** button,* *, to return without printing.*

5. Close the project without saving.

Driving Lesson 87 - Revision

Park and Read

At the end of every section you get the chance to complete one or more revision exercises to develop your skills and prepare you for your ECDL certification test. You should aim to complete the following steps without referring back to the previous lessons.

Manoeuvres

1. Open the project **revision** that you created earlier.

*An up-to-date model copy of the **revision** project is available in the data files folder **Training**. This is named **section12 revision**. If you would like to use this, open the project and save it as **revision** in the main data files folder.*

2. Display the **Print Screen** for the **Gantt Chart** and examine the print preview. Step through the print using the navigation buttons.
3. From within **Page Setup**, add the **Project Title** as a centred **Header**.
4. Add your **Manager Name** as a left-aligned **Footer** and **Page Number** as a right-aligned **Footer**.
5. Select to print the first **6** columns of the task sheet on every page.
6. Select to print notes and make sure no blank pages are printed.
7. Change all margins to **1.4 cm**.
8. Preview the project to see the effect the changes have had on the appearance of the schedule.
9. Scale the project to be printed on one page.
10. Print the project (or click **Back** to return without printing).
11. Display the **Network Diagram** view for this project. Then print a scaled 4 pages wide by 1 page tall copy (or click **Back** to return without printing).
12. Return to the **Gantt Chart** view, save the project and close it.

*A sample project named **section12 revision complete** can be found in the **Revisions** folder within the data files. You can use this to compare your work against a model solution.*

*Now complete the **Record of Achievement Matrix** at the back of the guide. You should only move on when confident with the topics and features described in this section.*

Section 13
Project Reporting

By the end of this section you should be able to:

Produce a report

Work through the **Driving Lessons** in this section to gain an understanding of the above features.

For each **Driving Lesson**, read all of the **Park and Read** instructions and then, if applicable, perform the numbered steps of the **Manoeuvres**. Complete the **Revision** exercise(s) at the end of the section to test your knowledge.

Driving Lesson 88 - Producing Reports

Park and Read

It is always a good idea to keep everyone involved in a project up-to-date on its progress. To help communicate the most important aspects of your plan to others, *Project* features the ability to easily print different types of **report**.

*Reports provide a brief, graphical overview of a project. These are ideal for communicating project progress in situations where the detail of a **Gantt Chart** or **Network Diagram** are unsuitable (e.g. a quick progress review meeting).*

Manoeuvres

1. Open the project **movie** that you created earlier.

*An up-to-date model copy of the **movie** project is available in the data files folder **Training**. This is named **section13 movie**. If you would like to use this, open the project and save it as **movie** in the main data files folder.*

2. Display the **REPORT** tab and click the **Dashboards** button in the **View Reports** group.
3. Select **Project Overview**. A handy report is shown that includes details about the project's progress, upcoming milestones and any late tasks.

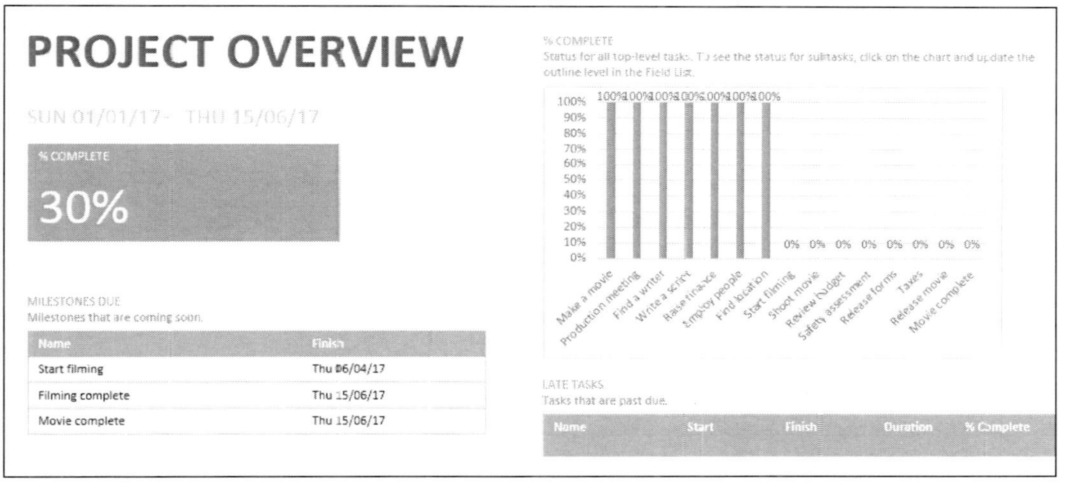

*You can print reports in the same way as you learned to print **Gantt Charts** and **Network Diagrams** earlier.*

4. Display the **FILE** tab and then click **Print** to see a preview of the report. This is how the report will appear if printed.
5. Click the **Back** button, , to return without printing.

Driving Lesson 88 - Continued

6. Display the **REPORT** tab again and click **Dashboards**. This time, create a **Burndown** report. This shows the tasks and "effort" used by a project

7. Display the **REPORT** tab again and click **Dashboards**. This time, create a **Cost Overview** report. This shows the money your project is costing you.

8. Display the **REPORT** tab again and click **Resources**. Click **Resource Overview** to create a report showing all of your project's resources and the work you have scheduled for them.

9. Display the **REPORT** tab again and click **Costs**. Click **Resource Cost Overview** to create a report showing resources and their cost to the project.

10. Display the **REPORT** tab again and click **In Progress**. Click **Critical Tasks** to create a report showing all of the important tasks on the critical path.

11. Try experimenting and creating some of the other report types available. Consider how each could be useful for communicating your project's status.

*The **REPORT TOOLS - DESIGN** tab features a number of chart formatting options. For example, you can change report fonts, colours, effects and even insert custom images, shapes and text boxes.*

12. Create a **Project Overview** report again.

13. Finally, try clicking each element on the chart and notice the tabs that appear on the **Ribbon**.

*You can move the parts of a report to new locations by simply clicking and dragging them. You can also resize charts and tables and customise the data they show using the **DRAWING TOOLS**, **TABLE TOOLS** and **CHART TOOLS** tabs that appear on the **Ribbon**.*

14. Feel free to explore and try the various report formatting tools available.

15. When you are finished, click on the **Status Bar** to view the **Gantt Chart** again.

*Project maintains one report at a time which you can view by clicking on the **Status Bar**. This "active" report is automatically kept up-to-date and will immediately show changes made to the project.*

16. Save the **movie** project and close it.

Driving Lesson 89 - Revision

Park and Read

At the end of every section you get the chance to complete one or more revision exercises to develop your skills and prepare you for your ECDL certification test. You should aim to complete the following steps without referring back to the previous lessons.

Manoeuvres

1. Open the project **revision** that you created earlier.

*An up-to-date model copy of the **revision** project is available in the data files folder **Training**. This is named **section13 revision**. If you would like to use this, open the project and save it as **revision** in the main data files folder.*

2. Create a **Resource Overview** report. How many hours of work do the **Technicians** have remaining?
3. Create a **Task Cost Overview** report. Which part of the project costs the most amount of money to complete?
4. Create a **Critical Task** report. How many critical tasks are left to complete?
5. Finally, create a **Project Overview** report. Notice that there are two milestones due and the task **Do the move** is **81%** complete.
6. Preview and print the **Project Overview** report.
7. Return to the **Gantt Chart** view.
8. Mark tasks **20**, **21** and **22** as **100% Complete**.
9. Mark task **24** as **50% Complete**.
10. Using a button on the **Status Bar**, return to the **Project Overview** report and notice that it has been automatically updated.
11. Return to the **Gantt Chart** view, save the project and close it.
12. Close *Project*.

*A sample project named **section13 revision complete** can be found in the **Revisions** folder within the data files. You can use this to compare your work against a model solution.*

*Now complete the **Record of Achievement Matrix** at the back of the guide. You should only move on when confident with the topics and features described in this section.*

Answers

Driving Lesson 9

1. The creation and planning of the project; the management of the schedule; the communication of the project information.
2. A project plan is not static. Once the project starts, it is important to continually track real-world progress and review, adjust and improve the project plan accordingly. Managing projects involves constantly balancing work, time, resources and costs.
3. Resources are the people, materials and equipment needed for a project.
4. A Gantt Chart is a type of bar chart that visualises a project and shows tasks as horizontal bars on a timeline. Each bar is a task, and the start, end and length of the bar indicates its duration.
5. Project start and end dates can be entered on the Project Information dialog box (click Project Information on the PROJECT tab).
6. Project properties can be entered on the Properties dialog box (on the File tab, select Info, click Project Information and then Advanced Properties).
7. A 24 hour day can be selected on the Project Information dialog box. Calendar options can then be set using the Change Working Time button available on the PROJECT tab.

Driving Lesson 24

1. A task in *Project* is any activity that needs to be accomplished within a specific period of time.
2. Automatic scheduling (Auto Scheduled).
3. All tasks take time to complete. This time is known as the task's duration and can be specified in months, weeks, days, hours and minutes.
4. If a task's duration is estimated, it appears with a question mark, ?
5. <Insert>
6. Place the mouse pointer over the required row number on the Row Heading Bar and click once to select it. Then press <Delete> to remove the task. Alternatively, you can right-click a task and select <Delete>.
7. Simply click and drag the task row number upwards or downwards.
8. Select the task's name by clicking it once and enter new text. This will overtype the original name.
9. You can split the task into two or more stages.
10. Milestones are used to mark the start or end of important events in the life of a project. They have a duration of 0 days.
11. Notes can be attached to tasks to add a little more detail beyond what is shown on the Task List and Gantt Chart.
12. You can add a hyperlink to a task to link it to another file or web page.

Notes

Record of Achievement Matrix

The **Record of Achievement** matrix can be used to measure progress through this guide. This is a learning reinforcement process - you judge when you are competent.

Three tick boxes are provided for each lesson. Column 1 should be ticked for **no knowledge** of the subject or topic covered, 2 for **some knowledge**, and 3 for **competent**. A section is only complete when you have ticked column 3 for all lessons.

Tick the Relevant Boxes **1**: No Knowledge **2**: Some Knowledge **3**: Competent

Section	No.	Driving Lesson	1	2	3
1 Getting Started	1	Project Management			
	2	Microsoft Project			
	3	The Project Screen			
	4	The Ribbon			
	5	Custom Views			
	6	Help			
	7	Project Information			
	8	Working Times			
2 Project Files	10	Saving a Project			
	11	Closing a Project			
	12	Opening a Project			
3 Tasks	14	Identifying Tasks			
	15	Adding Tasks			
	16	Inserting or Deleting Tasks			
	17	Moving or Copying Tasks			
	18	Editing Task Names			
	19	Task Durations			
	20	Splitting Tasks			
	21	Milestones			
	22	Notes			
	23	Hyperlinks			
4 File Formats & Templates	25	Saving with a New Name			
	26	Exporting a Project			
	27	Creating a Template			
	28	Saving a Template			
	29	Using a Template			
5 Subtasks	31	Creating Subtasks			
	32	Displaying Subtasks			
	33	Recurring Tasks			
6 Linking Tasks	36	Task Dependencies			
	37	Predecessors & Successors			
	38	Finish-To-Start Links			

Tick the Relevant Boxes **1**: No Knowledge **2**: Some Knowledge **3**: Competent

Section	No.	Driving Lesson	1	2	3
	39	Start-To-Start Links			
	40	Finish-To-Finish Links			
	41	Start-To-Finish Links			
	42	Gantt Chart Links			
	43	Task Information Links			
	44	Changing Links			
	45	Maintaining Links			
	46	Best Practice			
	47	Adjusting Zoom Levels			
7 Lag, Lead & Elapsed Time	50	Lag Time			
	51	Lead Time			
	52	Elapsed Time			
8 Constraints & Deadlines	55	Task Constraints			
	56	Fixed Constraints			
	57	Flexible Constraints			
	58	Schedule Conflicts			
	59	Deadlines			
9 Resources & Costs	62	Creating Resources			
	63	Costs			
	64	Assigning Work Resources			
	65	Assigning Materials/Costs			
	66	Dealing with Change			
	67	Effort-Driven Scheduling			
10 Project Monitoring	70	Monitoring a Project			
	71	Critical Path			
	72	Creating a Baseline			
	73	Updating Task Progress			
	74	Updating Project Progress			
	75	Rescheduling Work			
	76	Progress Lines			
11 Project Views	78	Gantt Chart Navigation			
	79	Task List Columns			
	80	Sorting and Filtering Tasks			

Tick the Relevant Boxes **1**: No Knowledge **2**: Some Knowledge **3**: Competent

Section	No.	Driving Lesson	1	2	3
	81	Network Diagrams			
12 Printing	83	Print Preview			
	84	Print Settings			
	85	Advanced Page Setup			
	86	Printing			
13 Project Reporting	88	Producing Reports			

Index